T0010877

What Is Church?

Endorsements

What is Church? is a timely, thoughtful, and thought-provoking look at God's heart and design for the Church, relevant to the skeptic, the disillusioned and the faithful alike. During a time of upheaval in the church and the world, Dub graciously leads us through a deep and interactive exploration of the scriptures and guides us to find our place in God's glorious story for His people. Whether your experience with the church has brought healing or harm, this book will challenge and inspire you to revisit what God intended the Church to be – Love expressed in community. Filled with relatable anecdotes and practical applications, Dub reminds us, that despite her imperfections, a healthy Church is still hope for a hurting world. I personally found healing and hope in the pages of this book. Dive in. I believe you will too.

Heather Mercer, Co-Author of New York Times Bestselling
Memoir, *Prisoners of Hope: The Story of Our Captivity and
Freedom in Afghanistan*, Founder and President of Global Hope

Over the last two thousand years, empires and Fortune 500 companies have risen and fallen. But the church Jesus founded continues to grow and fill the earth, just as He promised. In *What is Church?* Pastor Dub does a fantastic job of getting to the heart of why. Let the words presented produce understanding, awe, and gratefulness within for the sacred privilege of being a part of God's eternal plan.

Jim Graff, Pastor of Faith Family Church
and President of the Significant Church Network

What is Church? A few years ago, to a Christian that might have seemed an insincere question. Today, our confidence is shattered. The Church we love has become known for judgmentalism, hypocrisy, and conflict. It's more than an image problem. In this book Dub Karriker challenges the reader to deconstruct our faltering understanding of the human institution of church so that we may rediscover what is genuine and eternal.

Dr. Bob Kretzu, United Methodist Pastor and Author of
Sam Edney & The First Camp Meeting

What is Church? has refreshed us in our lives in God's church. It is a strong reminder of the marvelous plan of God that is working in and through the Church, even with all her imperfections and humanness. You can't read this book without getting your toes bruised, but the gentleness and love with which Dub Karriker writes imparts faith and joy.

Michael and Gloria Cotten, Founders of AIM, Mercy Press,
and Authors of *When God Speaks* and *In The Beginning*

The Church is so important to our communities. How have we drifted away from our truth and focus? *What is Church?* is a critical read for a lover of Jesus Christ, or a questioning individual, and even one that has yet to believe. There could not be a timelier book. I would trust no one more to write *What is Church?* than Dub Karriker.

Dr. Wanda Boone, CEO and Founder of Pinnacle Community
Development Center/Together for Resilient Youth (T.R.Y.)

This is not a dry manual about an institution, but rather a lush personal inspection of the Creator's desires for his children both individually and corporately. This essential and clarifying book is for the faithful and the curious.

Karen Sleeth, Author, recently anthologized in
Hard to Find: An Anthology of New Southern Gothic

The reported decline of the church is no joke. It is happening in many places around the world today. But why, and what can we do about it? The institution that has stood so long was never supposed to be an institution in the first place! Dub Karriker's new book *What is Church?* addresses the source of the frustrations and disappointments many people experience when they encounter what passes for the church today, by reminding us of what God's plan for Jesus and His church has been all along. Addressing both biblical and historical contexts, *What Is Church?* provides hope through a rediscovered and revitalized community of God's people being who God created us to be.

Lonnie R. Nelson, Ph.D. Professor of Philosophy,
Hannibal-LaGrange University

Basing this work on scripture and tying it to history and current happenings, Dub Karriker addresses the issue of what truly is "Church." More importantly, he explores what is "The" Church. While *What is Church?* is great for individual readers, there are questions at the end of each chapter making it also profitable for group study.

Dr. David McLaughlin MA, MTS, D.Min.

This wonderful and inspiring book shows the true definition, the one foundation, and the importance of the church. Out of his vast experience Pastor Dub Karriker deals with the local and global church and provides many practical and personal insights. It will surely inform and empower the readers. I highly recommend obtaining a copy of *What is Church?*

Dr. Theodore Wesley Gudala, Director Mission Asia 2040

WHAT IS

CHURCH

Finding the
love of God
in the unique
community
of Jesus

DUB KARRIKER

NASHVILLE

NEW YORK • LONDON • MELBOURNE • VANCOUVER

What Is Church?

Finding the love of God in the unique community of Jesus

© 2024 Dub Karriker

All rights reserved. No portion of this book may be reproduced, stored in a retrieval system, or transmitted in any form or by any means—electronic, mechanical, photocopy, recording, scanning, or other—except for brief quotations in critical reviews or articles, without the prior written permission of the publisher.

Published in New York, New York, by Morgan James Publishing. Morgan James is a trademark of Morgan James, LLC. www.MorganJamesPublishing.com

Proudly distributed by Publishers Group West®

Morgan James BOGO™

A **FREE** ebook edition is available for you or a friend with the purchase of this print book.

CLEARLY SIGN YOUR NAME ABOVE

Instructions to claim your free ebook edition:
1. Visit MorganJamesBOGO.com
2. Sign your name CLEARLY in the space above
3. Complete the form and submit a photo of this entire page
4. You or your friend can download the ebook to your preferred device

ISBN 9781636982199 paperback
ISBN 9781636982205 ebook
Library of Congress Control Number: 2023937765

Cover Design & Interior Design by:
Christopher Kirk
www.GFSstudio.com

Morgan James PUBLISHING Builds with... Habitat for Humanity Peninsula and Greater Williamsburg

Morgan James is a proud partner of Habitat for Humanity Peninsula and Greater Williamsburg. Partners in building since 2006.

Get involved today! Visit: www.morgan-james-publishing.com/giving-back

Unless otherwise noted Scripture quotations are from the ESV® Bible (The Holy Bible, English Standard Version®), copyright © 2001 by Crossway, a publishing ministry of Good News Publishers. Used by permission. All rights reserved. The ESV text may not be quoted in any publication made available to the public by a Creative Commons license. The ESV may not be translated in whole or in part into any other language.

Scripture quotations marked (NIV) are taken from the Holy Bible, New International Version®, NIV®. Copyright © 1973, 1978, 1984, 2011 by Biblica, Inc.™ Used by permission of Zondervan. All rights reserved worldwide. www.zondervan.comThe "NIV" and "New International Version" are trademarks registered in the United States Patent and Trademark Office by Biblica, Inc.™

Scripture taken from the New King James Version®. Copyright © 1982 by Thomas Nelson. Used by permission. All rights reserved.

George Barna quote from https://www.barna.com/research/barna-survey-examines-changes-in-worldview-among-christians-over-the-past-13-years/ Copyright © 2009 by Barna Group Inc. Used by permission. All rights reserved.

Excepts taken from Standing Strong Through the Storm, compiled by Paul Estabrooks and Jim Cunningham © Open Doors International. Used by permission. All rights reserved. Visit OpenDoorsUS.org for other stories from persecuted Christians.

Mark Hackett quote is from his blog. https://www.markhackett.com/ Copyright © 2017-2022 Mark Hackett. All rights reserved.

For My Mom
Louise Karriker
Librarian in Heaven

Table of Contents

Foreword

There's a lot of heart behind this book. I first met Dub Karriker over twenty years ago after I had been given "the left foot of fellowship" at another church in the city in which we both live, Durham, North Carolina. Dub was the co-pastor of a healthy and growing church just a few miles away, which kindly welcomed our frazzled family. Before long I was meeting regularly with Dub and the church's founding pastor, trying to figure out where God was leading in those uncertain days. The church I serve today, Peace Church, was planted during those conversations.

Dub understands that a heart for God also means a heart for others. Whether it was for me as a hurting pastor coming out of a dysfunctional situation or for people of different ethnicities and cultures in our racially diverse city in the American South, Dub has consistently acted upon the love of Jesus in practical and transformational ways. His work in ministry, which has included extensive work in missions and "tent-making" endeavors where he was self-supporting for the good of the church, have demonstrated a faithfulness and preparedness "in season and out of season." **II Timothy 2:4**. His love for the poor in our community and "the least of these," **Matthew 25:40**, is very much after

God's heart. His musical gifts round out the experience of a life lived not only in working in the church, in business, and the community, but also in worship.

The best work of ministry is done when no one is looking (but God). Pastors who take the time to visit the sick and attend to their needs, who answer the phone call at home to counsel those going through difficult marriages, and give the extra hours to shepherd those who are just coming to faith may not be noticed much this side of heaven, but their reward will be great. Dub is in their company, a man who serves, not for attention, but because he is called by God and can't stay away. You'll find these convictions not only represented here, but also turned into vital questions that encourage our own relationship with God.

It is this relationship that informs so much of this book, a down-to-earth keeping company with Jesus in which prayer plays a vital part. For several years I participated with Dub in Durham Ministers in Prayer, a group of pastors praying for change that only God could bring. The group is as diverse as our city, and Dub served faithfully on its leadership team (and if the truth be told, attended more frequently than I did, even though I write books on prayer). They also have a practice of doing prayer walks in difficult places, where shootings or violence occurred, in an effort to bring light into the darkness. Many churches, large and small, of multiple backgrounds, joining together to simply show the love of Jesus, manifesting His presence as one Body made up of many parts. It is in looking to Jesus and loving Him above all else that we find our place and our peace together. Dub understands this well. In one point in this book, he recalls a moment where another believer, displaced from her country, was welcomed and loved by his own church family. *"Church that morning,"* he writes, *"didn't have anything to do with our location, our liturgy, our cultural norms and standards, or anything else. We simply focused on the essentials, Jesus and a few of His followers met together and worshiped Him. He does the rest."*

This is simple but not simplistic, the experience of believers across time and culture. Where Jesus is lifted up the Spirit moves in unity and draws us near to the Father's heart. This book is marked with that kind of expectant faith; that God came to be known, and that knowing Him is not only the best thing that can ever happen to us, but also the beginning of the greatest adventure imaginable.

What Is Church? invites you on that adventure. It doesn't simply tell you about it. It engages you and beckons you in, humbly and honestly. Dub relates much of his own journey of discovery of God's goodness, including unexpected places where he found himself questioning and struggling with our natural human tendency to judge God. But God did not leave him there; nor will He us. This book contains multiple, engaging, and original illustrations about what it means to know Jesus and be part of His church, drawing from a lifetime of experience in relationship and ministry.

Each brief chapter includes several helpful questions to aid in applying the content and moving forward with it in the ways God may be specifically leading you. You'll also find Dub's conclusions to be thoroughly buttressed with Scripture along with fascinating data woven throughout. This book works well for either personal or group study and discussion. Keep reading! The conclusions you reach as you do will not be Dub's alone, but those that God leads you to as you walk through these pages with Him. *"The Lord makes firm the steps of the one who delights in him,"* **Psalm 37:23 NIV.** I conclude these words with a prayer that God will lead you ever deeper into His joy.

Dr. James Banks, bestselling Author of *Prayers for Prodigals*, Pastor, and Church Planter

Acknowledgments

This is my first book. It feels like a miracle it is being published. As miracles are divine domain my first acknowledgment must be to Almighty God, the original Author and Creator of all good things. Jesus is my Savior, my Lord, my Master, and my Friend. His Church is the reflection of His work and His glory. If there is anything good or worthy of praise it belongs to Him. In humility, I submit this work and the work of all those who have been part of its creation for His approval.

Beyond what is most important, there is a whole host of people and organizations that I need to thank. My wife Pam must come next because she is a literal saint. She loves Jesus dearly and as a result she has put up with me for more than forty-four years. She deserves much more than a brief "thank you" in a book. It isn't much compensation. When you see her, please know she's an amazing kind of special. This book would not exist without her. Neither would I. Thanks babe.

I have a wonderful family that has taught me much about what the family of God should be. My parents and grandparents are gone but their legacy of faith and courage lives on. My in-laws are among the finest people that I know. Our daughter Marie has given us an understanding and appreciation of what God sees in His children. My sister and brother-in-law, nieces, nephews, aunts, uncles, and their families on both sides of the marital line are all very near and dear to me. You'll see family throughout this book, both in the natural and the spiritual. I am sometimes amazed at just how richly blessed I am.

I want to thank Morgan James Publishing for seeing the merit in my book and making the decision to publish it. I especially want to thank Terry Whalin, Acquisitions Editor, for first reading and recommending my book to the Morgan James team. Thanks also to the Founder, David Hancock, Jim Howard, Tom Dean, Author Relations Manager, Gayle West, Wes Taylor, Naomi Chellis, Lisa Hollingsworth, and everyone else that has been involved with the design, production, publication, and distribution.

Many people have read, edited, made recommendations, suggested improvements, and provided endorsements for the manuscript. Thank you to Karen Sleeth for your textual recommendations and for the gift of your professional editing expertise. Thanks also to James Banks, Heather Mercer, Jim Graff, Wanda Boone, David McLaughlin, Lonnie Nelson, Michael & Gloria Cotten, Bob Kretzu, Rachael Jones, Daniel Sigmon, Dr. Theodore Wesley Gudala, and everyone else that played a part in bringing the manuscript to life.

One of my early jobs was Church Youth Worker. I've been invested in children, teens, and young adults for most of my life and ministry. My views on Church have largely been shaped by people much younger than me. Their passion, energy, influence, and unvarnished insight keeps me grounded and humble. Through their eyes and experiences, I see the relationship of Jesus and His Church not only in history or just in my own life, but also very much as it is in the present and as we walk together into the future. I want to thank all the children, teens, youth groups, youth gatherings, young adults, interns, foster kids, godchildren, and dear young friends that have taken the time to share their thoughts, ideas, and their lives with me over the years. War

Cry, Sponge, Love Shack, VBS, and all the others, I love you and thank you so very much.

My home church, Christian Assembly Church of Durham, NC is the most supportive group of friends and family that I could have. Special thanks posthumously to my longtime pastor and friend, Paul Gordon and to his ageless widow, my mother in the Lord, Ernie Gordon. I learned my deep love of the Church from them. Thanks too to Jim & Beth Stanfield. They took a young, slightly wild, and clueless couple, and showed them all that it means to love people with abandon and follow Jesus whole-heartedly. I also want to thank my friends from Durham Ministers In Prayer. For more than twenty years it has been my privilege to pray once a week with brothers and sisters across generations, denominations, racial, ethnic, and cultural lines, and tear down every other uninspired wall of division for the good of the people in our city and beyond.

I am blessed with many friends and partners in far-flung places of the world that simply love Jesus and His Church. Some are mentioned in this book. Many cannot have their names or locations in print because their lives and their work are too important to disclose publicly. You know who you are. Thank you for teaching me what it means to follow Jesus courageously, to be Christ's Church no matter the culture or the opposition, and to love a broken, hurting, and dying world enough to tell people everywhere the Good News no matter the personal cost. I'm grateful for the inspiration, training, tireless work, and support Open Doors International provides for these dear brothers and sisters and for those who labor in the field. Thanks for going and for staying.

There are honestly too many people I need to thank. I know I'm going to miss some of you that are very important and dear to me. Please forgive me for the omission. You will always have a place in my heart and in this book. Please know I love and appreciate you. More importantly, rest assured the Lord knows who you are. Because He is good, He will no xxii | **WHAT IS CHURCH?**

doubt cover for my inadequacy. You will receive your reward, whether I or anyone else knows about it or not.

Finally, I am honored that you are reading this book. I am grateful to you all. Thank you for investing in my life and my work.

Preface

Col. 1:18. *"And He (the Lord Jesus Christ)*
is the head of the body, the church."

I have a confession. I love the Church. I love the Church in all her various forms and permutations. I love the Church in every nation. I love the Church in all her humility and in all her glory. I love the Church. She is beautiful to me.

Why do I love the Church? Because I love Jesus and Jesus loves His Church. I love her because Jesus is coming back for the Church and she will be without spot or wrinkle, holy and blameless. Is she perfect? No, not yet. But that makes her all the more attractive to Jesus and to me, because I am not perfect yet either. One day the Church will all see Him together and we will be like Him. But that day is not yet. This is one big reason why I love Him. He loves me now, not just in the future when I am finally perfect.

He loves me, He chose me, and He saved me when I was foolish, and weak, and sinful, and dead in my trespasses and sins. He saved me, not by works of righteousness that I have done but according to His mercy, through the washing of regeneration and renewal of the Holy Ghost. He made me alive again with all the saints and He changed me. He transformed me by the washing of water with the Word. He is my King. He is the head of the Church, His body. I belong to the Church and I love her. I could no more despise her or leave her than I could leave Jesus.

God knows we need the Church. The world is in upheaval. The COVID-19 pandemic and wars that may go nuclear and expand into a global conflict are reshaping nations, institutions, cultures, and people. Evil is rampant and running amok like a spoiled child with a fully automatic weapon. The Church of Jesus Christ is not immune (pardon the unintended COVID pun) from the shaking of these days. If you are a believer in Jesus and you are familiar with the Bible you shouldn't be surprised. God certainly did not hide any of this from us.

Hebrews 12:22-29, *But you have come to Mount Zion and to the city of the living God, the heavenly Jerusalem, and to innumerable angels in festal gathering, and to the church of the firstborn who are enrolled in heaven, and to God, the judge of all, and to the spirits of the righteous made perfect, and to Jesus, the mediator of a new covenant, and to the sprinkled blood that speaks a better word than the blood of Abel. See that you do not refuse him who is speaking. For if they did not escape when they refused him who warned them on earth, much less will we escape if we reject him who warns from heaven. At that time his voice shook the earth, but now he has promised, "Yet once more I will shake not only the earth but also the heavens." This phrase, "Yet once more," indicates the removal of things that are shaken—that is, things that have been made—in order that the things that cannot be shaken may remain. Therefore, let us be grateful for receiving a kingdom that cannot be shaken, and thus let us offer to God acceptable worship, with reverence and awe, for our God is a consuming fire.*

Christians and non-Christians alike are watching the monumental shaking that is occurring in the church worldwide. Scandal after scandal comes to light. The shaking is having a profound effect. Many Christians are reexamining their faith as some of the forces they see at work in the church don't match what they've been taught to believe and yet long to experience. That's understandable. Jesus had much to say about religious hypocrisy and it wasn't good.

No matter how much questioning of what church is and whether what we have known in the past remains valid today, the scripture is clear that at least in God's heart, mind, and will His Church is critical to people's lives, their purpose on earth, and indeed to the well-being of the World. If you are a believer, a follower, a disciple of Jesus I hope you are seeking, reading, praying, and fasting, asking God for direction in all matters. I also hope you're listening for the Lord's voice because He is very much alive, active, and involved. He continues to speak to His people and to the world if we care to listen.

Amid worldwide upheaval, believers and non-believers alike are asking questions and one in particular. What is Church? Thank you for taking the time to read this book. I hope to help you resolve your longing for answers, truth, meaning, and belonging by plumbing the depths of divinely revealed knowledge. Each individual personal experience of church is quite another thing. My prayer is that you will discover both the truth and the life of Church as Jesus intends.

Where to begin? For the purpose of this book, you will see the title word expressed in two ways. Church with a capital "C" represents the global Church of Jesus Christ. This Church consists of all true disciples of Jesus from the time of its inception until His return. When you see church with a little "c" it represents individual churches, groups of people that gather in the name of Jesus whether they be individuals, families, home meetings, local congregations, denominations, networks, small or large associations. At no point will church refer to a building as there is no association with such a reference in the Bible.

Let's start with a basic question that is designed for the individual reader. What kind of church or churches do you know? There are many kinds of churches. Denominational/Non, Evangelical (whether in doctrine, philosophy, politics, works, or any combination), Mainline, Independent. Charismatic, Pentecostal, Spirit-filled. Traditional/Non. Dead or alive. True or false. Biblically literal or not so much. Conservative or Liberal. Diverse or Homogenous. God centered, God powered, or people centered, people powered. Mega, large, average size, small, micro, nano.

Next, what kind of church does God want His people to associate with? Perhaps the more pertinent question is this: Do I need to be involved in a church at all? Maybe this is the big question that led you to read this book. As the time of Jesus' return draws near, God is encouraging and perhaps even prodding us to seek Him and make a choice. It's evident to me that this is happening not just individually and among nuclear families. By His Word and by His Spirit God is challenging every individual, family, generation, congregation, church, denomination, and association to reconsider our course in light of His revealed will. You can't help but do that when something you have depended on for guidance, structure, fellowship, comfort, identity, and meaning has been exposed to the light and shaken to the core.

That leads us back to the question posed by this book. What is Church? By that I mean, what is Church as God intends? Further, what are individuals and congregations not only called to DO individually and together, but what are we supposed to BE before God, before people, and in the world? How can individuals and the Church truly be ministers of reconciliation and witnesses of Jesus Christ as the Bible instructs?

Thank you for taking this journey with me. Let's dig in together.

Chapter 1

"Let the little children come to me." ~ Jesus

The search for Church is not a new inquiry for me. I grew up in a large United Methodist Church in El Dorado, Arkansas. I say large because that is the way is seemed to me as a child. By today's megachurch standards it would barely be a drop in the puddle outside the door. But it was the largest Methodist Church in an area that was inundated with Methodism and other mainline Protestant traditions.

In my childhood, church was mostly about the building and what went on in it. It was wonderful and sometimes mystifying. I have all sorts of fond memories of things that occurred in that building. There was the fellowship hall where we regularly had delicious potluck dinners. The sheer volume of food and the variety of goodies always exceeded my wildest expectations. We even had a church dietician although I'm pretty sure she barely managed anything except the meals that were sometimes prepared in the large commercial kitchen onsite. The tastes and smells were glorious and untamed.

2 | WHAT IS CHURCH?

I remember a men's (and apparently boy's) meeting where the guest speaker was Terry Bradshaw. At the time he was the quarterback at Louisiana Tech just fifty miles down the road in Ruston, LA. I remember he was funny and impressive as he spoke about football and faith. Little did we know that we were entertaining a future NFL Football Hall of Fame quarterback. Of course, he did play for the Pittsburgh Steelers against everyone in South Arkansas' favorites, the Dallas Cowboys. He and the Steelers would break my heart more than once in big games. It's OK Terry. Jesus forgives you. I guess I can too.

We had wonderful Sunday School teachers. My favorite was Mr. Jimmy Synott. He was about eighty years old, dressed the part, and was about as uncool as any human being could be. But he loved us and we loved him back. His quiet and confident faith in Jesus made a big impression on me.

The sanctuary was a large, impressive place framed by very tall, intricate stained-glass windows of Bible characters and stories. I studied them carefully sitting in church. The images I saw and learned there still influence my impressions of people and stories in the Bible today. The front of the sanctuary was dominated by a huge pipe organ. It was massive and impressive. When the organist kicked in the trumpet en chamade everyone jumped in their seats! It was startling and awesome.

I mostly sat in the balcony, first with my parents and then later with my friends. It was a great place to observe the goings on. Our pastors were friendly and their sermons were folksy and not too long. They rotated every few years so we never got bored hearing the same messages. It was important that they were on time. After all, we had to beat the Baptists to the restaurants after church. We took communion once a quarter, first at the altar and later as the ushers passed plates with unsalted crackers and grape juice down the rows.

I had a fun childhood in a church filled with many fond memories. In that sense, you could say I grew up Christian. It was the norm for me and most of my friends. Almost everyone I knew shared similar experiences. That was true across racial lines, which in my limited experience consisted mainly of black and white. Later I met and befriended a Jewish girl from the tiny local synagogue and became friends with some Catholic and Pentecostal kids. Still, they didn't seem so different from my Methodist, Baptist, and Presbyterian friends, even the girl from whatever an exotic and mysterious synagogue was.

These were my first understandings of church. It was a building. A place where good people gathered together once a week to shake hands, sing songs, listen to a Bible lesson, pass the plate, say the Lord's Prayer, sing the Doxology, join in a responsive reading of scripture, listen to good choral music, and hear messages about God. Then we went out to eat. Sometimes there was even a big meal at the church. I officially "joined the church" after taking a confirmation class at age twelve and participating in a little ceremony. My idea of church at that time was simple. Nice and tidy.

Then I became a teen. That's when the first nagging questions about life began to emerge in my adolescent brain. More on that later. For now, fast forward about forty years.

On a vacation more than a decade ago as I was actively pastoring our congregation I read a book by Kevin Roose titled, *The Unlikely Disciple.* (Grand Central Publishing) The author was raised in an unchurched, socially liberal, Quaker family. At the time the book was written a Barna poll indicated that a third of the author's contemporaries self-identified as born-again, evangelical Christians. As a university student Mr. Roose became curious as to what that meant.

On a quest for understanding he left Brown University for a semester and transferred to Liberty University to investigate what was for him a cross-cultural experience. He subsequently wrote a book about it. For the first time he examined the evangelical church in America, not based on what he had heard or read from others, but as an insider (although still an unbeliever). His account is enlightening, funny, and poignant. While the information presented is somewhat dated now it is a wonderful study of what the church looks like from an outsider's perspective.

On this same vacation my wife and I traveled in search of warmer surroundings. We visited Coral Ridge Presbyterian Church in Ft. Lauderdale, founded by Dr. D. James Kennedy, then pastored by thirty-seven-year-old Tullian Tchividjian, one of Billy Graham's grandsons. Dr. Kennedy, a respected elder of the Church, passed away in 2007. Tullian Tchividjian was called to pastor this well-established congregation in 2009, merging with another church in the process. He was elected in March and by our visit in July he was under severe public attack from six church members circulating a petition to all members demanding his removal on the grounds of deserting the heritage of Dr. Kennedy. Their chief complaints-downplaying the church's traditional pipe-organ accompanied hymns in favor of contemporary worship and bringing new people on staff.

During our visit the worship service was wonderful. We found the people welcoming and the presence of the Lord was evident. At the end of the service my wife and I spoke with Pastor Tchividjian. Then we prayed for him and encouraged him to hang in there. He did for a while. Unfortunately, he was deposed from the church and by his denomination in 2015 for a moral failure. That's another story but one that certainly has relevance to our theme.

The next Sunday we attended a small Assembly of God church in a rural town. The people were friendly and welcoming. We knew all the worship songs that were sung to recorded music. We shared the Lord's Supper. The message was about commitment and sharing the Gospel and while the pastor was sincere, it was a mess biblically. The pastor really seemed to have a desire to reach the people in his town for Jesus Christ, but the approach he described definitely needed some work.

In the sermon he was trying to encourage the congregation to boldly share their faith. Unfortunately, he used a personal story of a previous day's visit to McDonalds as an example of an effective gospel presentation. He told of an encounter with a woman he did not know that was in line in front of him placing an order. She was obviously having a very bad day. After she said something unkind to the person behind the counter he said, *"That's not very Christian of you. You need Jesus."* He made it clear to the congregation that he purposely spoke loudly enough for everyone in the restaurant to hear him and further that he intended his words as a public declaration of the gospel. The embarrassed woman was stunned into silence. She awkwardly stood there and glared at him as all other conversation in McDonalds ceased and all eyes turned toward the two of them. He then loudly said to her, *"Have a blessed day."*

I doubt she did.

If you reside in the Southern US, and/or are a Boomer like me, it may surprise you to learn that over half of the population of America is looking in on the church from the outside. In my mid-sized, Southern, former Bible Belt city on any given Sunday morning perhaps 15% of the population will be in church. Some attend sporadically, more have at least been to church at some point in their lives, and a growing number see no need for church at all.

Some see the church as their enemy. No wonder. The news is filled with headlines like the pastor of a church ironically named Faithful Word publicly stating that he was praying for the President…to die. Stories of church people's hypocrisy and misdeeds are common. What does that say about the state of the church and its relevance to society?

What is Church? Why do Christians gather on Sunday morning? What does this practice say about the people of God to the world? Is church just an archaic ritual that Christians follow for some reason? Is church relevant to people's lives today and to society? Why are there so many denominations? Why are churches so different? Is church just another secret, exclusive society? Is the non-profit, 501c3 corporation that we know as church in America really what Jesus bled and died to create? What does being a member of a church have to do with being a follower of Jesus Christ?

In the wake of the recent pandemic, with all the resources that are readily available to anyone with a smartphone or other electronic device connected to the internet, does physically gathering together even make sense or matter anymore? What is church supposed to be? What is its purpose?

I've barely scratched the surface. There are a lot of questions. You may have chosen this book because you have questions or concerns that I haven't mentioned. I've purposely chosen not to make this a book a litany of the ills of the Church. That's not helpful nor wise. Instead, I believe it is right to pursue the pure and unadorned truth for What is Church from the Word of God. In that endeavor, let's start from the beginning.

Reflections

Prepare for the journey – In the space below please note your concerns and disappointments with the Church.

_____

_____

_____

_____

_____

Now list questions that you hope to have answered over the course of this book.

_____

_____

_____

_____

Finally, make a note of your current feelings about Church if any. We'll revisit these at the end of our journey together.

_____

_____

_____

_____

Chapter 2

In the Beginning

When I was a teen, I started to question many things that I had no reason or inclination to think about as a child. One of those things was church. What is church? Why did we go? What were we there for? Why did we do the same thing every week? What is the goal? I didn't dare ask my parents. Church was settled in their minds. It's just what we did. Period. End of story. In fact, spiritual practice and religious belief questions seemed to irritate them. So where to go for answers?

Before Jesus, there was no Church as we know it now. For approximately 400 hundred years leading up to the incarnation of Christ the Jews had temple service, annual feasts and festivals, and synagogues where they gathered to worship God. Other religions had their own gatherings and practices. Religion and religious rituals were a normal part of everyday life, but the sense of a living God and His natural order were ancient stories, a religious heritage to be taught, learned, and repeated. Perhaps you can relate.

The Holy Scriptures the Jews possessed contained many references and prophecies of a coming Messiah who would save and deliver His people from all sorts of evil and oppression. That would be a welcome experience considering the harsh conditions of the world they lived in. But that was not their present reality. Those assurances were made and delivered a long time ago to their ancestors. Centuries passed and nothing remarkable seemed to be happening. Where was God in their gatherings or in the world?

Suddenly Jesus appeared claiming the title. He performed every one of the supernatural works that they believed only the Messiah could do. He preached good news of the Kingdom of God on earth and performed miracles as evidence. It was a revelation. Everything they knew began to change. Through His miraculous birth, remarkable life, painful death, and unprecedented resurrection Jesus established the promised new covenant between God and mankind with His own blood. He opened the door for people to experience a new, unfamiliar, loving relationship with God as their Father. The salvation that Jesus provided was not only individual. He established a close community centered on faith in God and relationship with Him. This new family of believers would be no longer focused on human bloodlines and genealogy, religion and rituals, but on direct relationship with God as sons and daughters, brothers and sisters, through surrender to His Son, Jesus Christ the Redeemer, Savior, King, Lord.

Jesus didn't begin his life and ministry talking about establishing a new enterprise or organization called "the church." He took up the trade of carpenter. As far as we know He ran His business as a sole proprietor to support his mother, brothers, and sisters. All the while His real work, His mission, was not to simply establish or run a successful business or even a new religious organization. He pursued a greater purpose.

Jesus appeared with the message that people should repent of their sins because the Kingdom of God had come to earth. He was sent from Heaven, born of a virgin, lived the life of a perfect human being, sacrificed Himself as the Lamb of God to atone for our sins, and rose from death and the grave to make a way for all people, Jew and Gentile, to freely come to God the Father. He gathered disciples, initially hundreds of them and later thousands, eventually millions more. It was only toward the end of His life and ministry that He began to speak to His disciples about the Church, His Church.

There's only one source that we can reliably use to determine what Jesus said, what He did, and what He intended to accomplish regarding the Church. The Holy Bible. **John 1:1**, *"In the beginning was the Word, and the Word was with God, and the Word was God."* Jesus and the written Word of God in the Bible are indivisible. Therefore, the Bible is the central and only authoritative source for our investigation of "What is Church?"

I know what I am about to state is somewhat controversial, but I believe it needs to be said. The Bible is not God. It is the written Word of God. Please don't misunderstand my assertion or my intent. I believe the Bible is inerrant, divinely inspired, God-breathed. I fully agree with the following statement. *"All Scripture is given by inspiration of God, and is profitable for doctrine, for reproof, for correction, for instruction in righteousness, that the man of God may be complete, thoroughly equipped for every good work."* **II Tim. 3:16-17 NKJV**

As delivered by God to men through the Holy Spirit, The Holy Bible is without error and unchallenged in its authority. The scriptures are the infallible rule of faith and practice for all Christians. No question. But the Bible itself is not God. Why do I feel the need to make that distinction and perhaps alienate some readers? Because the Bible can also be whatever one makes of it. Wisdom, comfort, counsel, truth. Weapon.

I am concerned that many Christians and churches have embraced the philosophy that God spoke once through Jesus and His Word and then eighty or so years after Jesus ascended into Heaven, God stopped speaking to His children. If that is true there is no longer a need for dependence on God or a responsibility to pursue a genuine relationship with Him. Under this philosophy, I often hear people pridefully and foolishly proclaiming that they live their lives, "by biblical principles." I've probably done it myself. In doing so I have witnessed many people make incredibly unwise decisions that have resulted in calamity, strife, and the ruin of both their lives and their relationships. What does living life "by biblical principles" even mean?

When we make the Bible out to be God what we are actually doing is making our own understanding, our own independent interpretation of the Bible to be God. Stop and read that again. When I live my life "by biblical principles" I'm not dependent on God anymore. What matters instead is my judgment of scripture and perhaps what my personally chosen experts say the Bible means. When my understanding or someone else's authority is set on the throne of God in my life all sorts of troubles ensue. It's easy to justify being mean, judgmental, and uncaring toward others when that's your philosophy. You don't need or value anyone else's input. This is the root of the unholy spiritual arrogance that is behind the Christian need to dominate others. It is a common reason for the lack of love and true compassion in some churches. As the old saying goes, "birds of a feather flock together."

A committed believer might not admit that's the philosophy they have adopted. They may never even think it is true. But when "living my life by biblical principles" is where we place our faith we have made ourselves equal with or even superior to God. That's more than a mistake. It is a grievous sin. It's called Pride with a capital "P". Any person or church that finds itself in this position should immediately humble themselves before God and repent.

Remember what the Lord says in **Is. 55:9**, *"For as the heavens are higher than the earth, so are My ways higher than your ways, And My thoughts than your thoughts."* That's not a lofty spiritual saying that is open to interpretation. God is simply stating an eternal truth that we'd do well to keep in mind as we humble ourselves in His presence.

Lest you think I am being too harsh and unreasonable consider the Pharisees in the story of Jesus. They're the bad guys, right? Mean, heartless, uncaring, lording over the people they are supposed to care for, lead, and guide. We forget that their original intent was to teach people to follow the Law as delivered by God, which is a good thing. It's not that the Law was bad or wrong. The problem is the Pharisees got carried away in their own understanding, interpretations, and explanations of what God commanded in the Law. They had their own way of living life "by biblical principles." They compiled their own writings of explanations and practices, written by their own experts in the Law, and held them in the same esteem as the Word of God itself. It produced the first "church split" and the first two denominations – the Pharisees and the Sadducees.

Pride is divisive. It is like a weed. It never stops expanding by itself. Jesus called it "the leaven of the Pharisees." Leaven permeates everything it touches. Pride caused the Pharisees and Sadducees to count their own thoughts as equal to God. Then, they enforced their interpretation of God's Word on the people they were intended to lead and inspire toward God through spiritual and physical manipulation and the exertion of unholy spiritual and organizational power over others. Any of that sound familiar in churches today?

No wonder the people of Jesus' time were looking for the Messiah to free them not just from the oppression of Rome, but also from the abuse of their religious overlords. The same yearning to be free is built into all of us by our Creator. We should not be surprised that we now number "exvangelicals, nones, and dones" as emergent social movements. We will always need Jesus to show us the Way, the Truth, and the Life! How else will we see His Church without the leaven of pride in our eyes? Jesus is continually working to free us from our sin and spiritual blindness by His Word and His Spirit. Are we in turn willing to surrender to Him? To study and accept what the Bible actually says, respond to His commands, and obey Him with our whole heart?

"Trust in the Lord with all your heart, and do not lean on your own understanding. In all your ways acknowledge him, and he will make straight your paths." **Proverbs 3:5-6**

We are not God. We cannot know all that God knows or fully understand His ways but we can seek and search out God's truth in His Word. God promises in **Jeremiah 29:13**, *"You will seek me and find me, when you seek me with all your heart."* The Bible, the Word of God, is only understood by those who are, to use a phrase that is biblical but out of fashion, born again, spiritual. The natural mind cannot understand God and His ways. **II Cor. 2:14**, *"The natural person does not accept the things of the Spirit of God, for they are folly to him, and he is not able to understand them because they are spiritually discerned."* **II Cor. 2:16**, *"For who has understood the mind of the Lord so as to instruct him?"* But we (speaking to faithful disciples of Jesus) have the mind of Christ."*

This knowledge gives us confidence. It is a solid foundation for establishing The Holy Bible as the only divine, reliable source in our search for "What is Church?" After all, what is the story of the Bible? God and His creation. God and humankind. Humankind's fall from grace. God's plan of salvation. It's the account of Jesus and our redemption. The Bible is the great story of God from the beginning of the world to His ultimate glory, the summing up of all things in Christ Jesus. We can trust what has been written for our edification. In other words, the answer to all our questions really is in The Bible. We just need the Holy Spirit to reveal it to us.

"One of these days some simple soul will pick up the Book of God, read it, and believe it. Then the rest of us will be embarrassed."
Leonard Ravenhill, British evangelist and author, 1907-1994

Take a minute now and ask Jesus to set you free of any misconceptions you have about the Bible and His Church. Ask the Holy Spirit to guide you into all truth as you study the Bible.

Reflections

Answer these questions as completely and honestly as possible:

How did you develop the beliefs and philosophy by which you live your life?

_____

_____

_____

How do you make decisions?

_____

_____

_____

Does truth matter? If so, what is your most trusted source (or sources) of truth?

_____

_____

_____

What is your honest assessment of your beliefs regarding church based on your answers to the questions above?

_____

_____

_____

_____

Chapter 3

The Church Belongs To Jesus

Colossians 2:8, *"See to it that no one takes you captive by philosophy and empty deceit, according to human tradition, according to the elemental spirits of the world, and not according to Christ."*

This instruction provides a solid platform for our investigation of What is Church? Let's commit together to put aside any extra-biblical philosophies, non-biblical traditions, generational, denominational, cultural, and world value influenced prejudices related to church and look first and foremost to Jesus Christ. Building on the Bible as our source, let's examine first what Jesus has to say about His Church. After all, the Church begins and ends with Jesus. Here's a conversation that Jesus had with His first disciples that includes the first mention of Church we find in the Bible.

Matthew 16:13-19, *"Now when Jesus came into the district of Caesarea Philippi, He was asking His disciples, "Who do people say that the Son of Man is?" And they said, "Some say John the Baptist; and others, Elijah;*

17

but still others, Jeremiah, or one of the prophets." He said to them, "But who do you say that I am?" Simon Peter answered, "You are the Christ, the Son of the living God." And Jesus said to him, "Blessed are you, Simon Barjona, because flesh and blood did not reveal this to you, but My Father who is in heaven. I also say to you that you are Peter (petros), and upon this rock I will build My church; and the gates of Hades will not overpower it. I will give you the keys of the kingdom of heaven; and whatever you bind on earth shall have been bound in heaven, and whatever you loose on earth shall have been loosed in heaven."

The Greek word Jesus used for Church is ekklēsia. We know from the Septuagint, the Greek translation of the OT, that this word was already in use among Jews for the "assembly of the called" of God. Previously Jesus also referred to His disciples as His family. He told His disciples in **Matt. 12:50** that *"whoever does the will of My Father in heaven is my brother and sister and mother."* Here for the first time Jesus refers to His family of faithful followers as His Church. He states His intention to build His Church and promises that nothing will stand in the way of the community, the family, of believers that follow Him, obey Him, and do His will. Jesus indicates that there are divine, powerful forces at work. Not even Hell itself will be able to withstand the force of the church of Jesus Christ. Hell's gates will be destroyed and Satan, the god of this world, will have his kingdom plundered by the Church. That's the victorious Church, the Bride of Christ, that Jesus will return for at the end of the age of man on the earth.

But I'm getting ahead of myself. We'll expand on this later. Before then, what else does Jesus have to say about the Church?

Matthew 18:17, *"If he refuses to listen to them, tell it to the church; and if he refuses to listen even to the church, let him be to you as a Gentile and a tax collector."*

To fully understand any single verse or selected segment of scripture, context is important. In this passage Jesus is instructing the first disciples (later called apostles) about spiritual family relations, i.e. Church matters. He encourages them to pursue and cultivate humility, teaches them regarding handling temptations to sin, encourages them to go after the lost, and tells them what to do when a Christian brother or sister sins against you. The Gentile and the tax collector are used here as illustrations of those who willfully and deliberately rebel against the revealed will of God.

It is hard for us today to relate to just how offended the first disciples were with Gentiles and tax collectors. They had been taught since they were children that such people are unclean or worse, traitors to God and to their people. Hearing these examples it would be easy for them to relate to the kind of serious offense and indignation that is stirred up when a Christian brother or sister sins against you. It is clear from His teaching that the church is made up of people, a spiritual family. The Church bears the responsibility of representing Christ on earth seriously, and does so, not by their own feelings of right and wrong and what is fair in human terms, but by the commands of His spoken and written word, under His authority, according to His will. It is the ongoing responsibility of the Church, the family of God to deal with and resolve these matters.

And that's it.

That's all Jesus specifically said about the Church before He went to Heaven. Now here we are today, 2000+ years later, trying to carry out the intentions of Jesus with regard to His Church in a world that is very different from the one that His disciples knew while He was here on earth. A great deal has happened since then. A lot has changed and is still changing. Did Jesus anticipate all of this? Is the Church still empowered by God and relevant today? Is the Church on track with what Jesus had in mind? Is what we know as church today the Church that Jesus intended to build and lead to victory?

This is important. If the Church, any church, truly belongs to Jesus we need to know if we are doing what He wants us to do; or more importantly if we are living as He intends us to live and becoming what He wants us to be. Wish as we may, Jesus isn't physically here to ask and answer our questions. How can we possibly know what He had or currently has in mind?

Fortunately, we have His thoughts, His works, His prayers, His heart, and His revealed will recorded in the Bible. There is a great deal of information about the Church in the rest of the New Testament. We can and should know what Jesus has in mind for His Church. Jesus invites us to ask, seek, and search. It is important that we do.

I should note that I was saved outside of church. Honestly, I don't remember ever hearing the actual Gospel presented in the church where I grew up. Maybe it was presented in some way, but it clearly didn't register with me. That wasn't part of my church experience in my childhood or into my teen years. In the summer of 1970, I went with my friends to a crusade that was held at the football stadium in my hometown. A traveling preacher named James Robison was holding nightly meetings and something unusual was happening.

There wasn't much to do in our small town, and I was interested to see what was bringing so many people to the stadium. As he preached that night, for the first time I really heard the message that I was a sinner and my sin separated me from God. I was convicted. I had certainly done more than my share of sinning in my short life and particularly that summer. I knew what he said was true and I felt very alone and disconnected from the God I was supposed to know. A deep sense of anguish and fear of God burned in the pit of my stomach. Then, he shared the Good News of Jesus and His work on the cross to bear my sin and shame. Jesus opened the door to forgiveness and the cleansing of my sin. All I had to do was confess and accept His offer of salvation and I would be saved.

I confessed every sin that came to my mind and asked Jesus to forgive me. I put my life in His hands and told Him I would follow and trust Him. Sure enough, everything changed. I felt free. I felt His love and acceptance. The guilt and fear disappeared. The anguish in my soul was replaced by peace and joy. I walked out of that stadium a changed young man. So did many of my friends. That began a life-long journey of faith and service to God that continues today, fifty+ years later. It also upended my childhood and adolescent understanding of church. This is what I hope to share with you.

Over the course of my life as a Christian I've experienced far too many people deeply hurt and wounded by the church, often meaning people that either are in leadership or those who carry influence within that sphere. Whether your experience has been inside the church or looking in from the outside, we've all had the opportunity to wonder what in the world is going on there? Believers and even the most disconnected and agnostic have had the thought, if Jesus is real how can He be so wonderful, and His church be so unlike Him?

As I've already mentioned, people have very different thoughts and ideas about church. Some of these ideas are good, and more are not. More importantly, it must be stressed that the Church should not really be practiced according to our thoughts and ideas at all, no matter how good and noble we believe our biblical understanding and intentions to be. The Church belongs to Jesus. Period. Full stop. It is not ours to tweak or mess with.

In **II Cor. 5:20** we who believe are called ambassadors of Christ, appointed by Jesus to represent His interests here on earth and give Him glory. In that capacity, His disciples have the responsibility to understand what the Church really is. Then we must expend our best effort to follow His will and take an active role in the Church that Jesus is building to assault the gates of Hell. Any other ideas we try to put into practice are foolish at best, sinful at worst, and could be downright harmful and dangerous to ourselves and others.

In **Matt. 16:18** Jesus tells Peter, *"I will build My Church…"* This means He isn't done yet. The apostles did not build the Church, set it in stone, and record the process in scripture. The Apostle Paul writes in **I Cor. 3:10**, *"According to the grace of God given to me, like a skilled master builder I laid a foundation, and someone else is building upon it. Let each one take care how he builds upon it."* The growth of the Church worldwide proves that Jesus is alive and that He is still building His Church.

Eph. 2:19-22, *"Now, therefore, you are no longer strangers and foreigners, but fellow citizens with the saints and members of the household of God, having been built on the foundation of the apostles and prophets, Jesus Christ Himself being the chief cornerstone, in whom the whole building, being fitted together, grows into a holy temple in the Lord, in whom you also are being built together for a dwelling place of God in the Spirit."*

No one can say in truth that they fully grasp the understanding of Church as Jesus intends or that they have established the perfect church. No human being rules the Church. There is no single perfect church, denomination, or church stream because Jesus is not finished with it, with us, yet. The amazing thing is that every single believer is not only part of His Church, but that each one has a part to play in its construction as we will soon see.

Before you begin the next chapter, please review the notes you have made so far. Then summarize your thoughts here. Use your summary for comparison as you read further to see if your understanding evolves and/or deepens.

Reflections

Write a brief summary of the Church Jesus is building as you now see it.

_____

_____

_____

_____

_____

_____

_____

What do you see as your place or responsibility in working with Jesus as He builds His Church?

_____

_____

_____

_____

_____

_____

Chapter 4

The West of Us

F
or the last thirty years or so the Lord has allowed me to spend a great
deal of time with brothers and sisters in many parts of the world. I've
had the privilege of being involved with believers and church leaders
in North America, the Caribbean, Latin America, Europe, Central Asia,
the Middle East, and one very brief visit to Africa. That's another story
for another time.

Taking advantage of the opportunity to observe and build relationships with Christians around the world has provided me with a wealth
of insight about Church and church practices that perhaps most Western
Christians have not been privileged to access. I've been involved with
mega churches, large churches, average size churches (the vast majority of
churches in America average 100 or less in attendance), small churches,
and house churches. I've been in churches both indoors and outdoors,
secret churches, intimate meetings with believers, sharing faith and meals
in homes. I've been both speaker and attendee at large and small conferences, led and participated in training sessions, prayer meetings, and
schools of various sorts. I have often worked with faithful translators to
assist with understanding. As a musician I have led and participated in

musical worship for all sorts of gatherings on large and small stages, in every sort of space, outdoors, and sitting painfully cross legged on the floor worshiping together silently so as not to draw the attention of nosy neighbors and hostile authorities.

I've been blessed to worship, train, and serve God together with brothers and sisters in Christ representing many different denominations, theological views, ethnicities, cultures, languages, and socio-economic conditions. On one level I think I have some understanding of just how blessed and privileged I am. Other times, and in the eyes of many of my Christian brothers and sisters, I sometimes realize that I remain incapable of grasping the breadth and depth of God's love and grace for those yet to believe, for me, and for His Church.

Since I retired from gainful employment much of my work is as the facilitator for a diverse network of churches, ministries, organizations, and believers that are focused on reaching a specific people group in Central Asia and the Middle East with the Good News. The people themselves are very dear to me. I am constantly amazed at their faith, boldness, and endurance. Just as Jesus promised, they suffer much. They live in harsh lands among people and governments that are hostile to the Gospel and to those that believe in Jesus. This is true even among their own families. They live with pressures, oppression, and dangers that I can barely imagine even though I know their stories. Still, the Church continues to grow in both numbers and spiritual maturity in every nation where they reside.

When we are able to meet in person we worship and pray together. We study God's Word. We discuss its application to our lives and real-world circumstances. We laugh, we hug, we dance, and we weep together. We share meals and stories. We encourage one another. As Jesus promised, in this community we experience a little bit of the Kingdom of God and His presence. We rejoice and are grateful. Even as I write this, tears well up in my eyes and my heart aches, longing to be with them once again. Though from vastly different worlds and with little in common, in Jesus we are a real family. The family of God.

Does that sound like Church to you? It does to me. But I think that is not what most American and other Western Christians experience. In fact, I know it isn't. My Twitter feed tells me so.

The church in the West is in crisis. In some areas of the world the Church is growing exponentially, but not in North America and Europe. For the last few hundred years we assumed the bulk of church expansion and thought was centered in Europe and North America. As a result, Western believers remain fairly ignorant of the fact that we're not the center of the church universe anymore, if we ever really were.

Every year tens of millions receive Christ, are baptized, and become disciples internationally while in Europe and North America the church is shrinking in numbers, in impact, in influence, and in faithfulness. In contrast, the 2020 Status of Global Christianity report from Gordon Conwell Theological Seminary found that both Africa and Latin America now have more Christians than Europe and the gap is getting wider.

According to the World Christian Encyclopedia (© Brill 2022), *"the number of Evangelicals in the world increased from 112 million in 1970 to 386 million in 2020. Globally, Evangelicalism is a predominantly non-White movement within Christianity, and is becoming increasingly more so, with 77% of all Evangelicals living in the Global South in 2020. This is up from only 7.8% in 1900."* Surprised? That's not what Americans see in the news.

I need to be transparent and admit that I'm not a fan of the term Evangelical with a capital "E" as a subset of Christianity. The evangel is the Good News, the Gospel of Jesus Christ. When Christians are following Jesus' command to go into all the world, preaching the Good News while making disciples of all the nations we are not Evangelical. That's merely being a faithful follower of Jesus. I'm not sure why we need a separate designation for that within the Church at large. That's why I prefer to use the term "faithful Christian" instead of Evangelical. The term itself is not accurate as surveys demonstrate that most Western Christians rarely share the Gospel with anyone. Now the term, "Evangelical" is associated with some of the worst tendencies of the church in the West. Therefore, it's use is just too pejorative for me. Sorry I digressed. Rant over. Back to the actual Good News.

The percentage of people in the world that remains without a Gospel presence continues to fall. In 1900, more than half the world's population was unevangelized (54.3%). By 2020, that percentage had decreased to 28.3%. Clearly God is moving, Jesus is saving, and His Church is expanding exponentially with new life as we await His return.

Meanwhile in the United States, a widely viewed Christian nation by the world at large where 64% of the population claims to be Christian, surveys by respected polling organizations including Gallup, Pew Research, Barna and others indicate staggering losses in church affiliation and attendance. According to Gallup in 2021 U.S. Church membership had fallen below the majority in the population (46%) for the first time. Is it any wonder that most American Christians are ignorant of the global growth of the Church and unaware that Christianity is growing at five times the rate of atheism worldwide? That's the kind of news you won't see in the world's media.

While the number of people claiming any faith at all is dropping steadily in America, as a retired pastor I am very concerned for those who claim to be faithful believers and yet do not participate in church or share their faith with nonbelievers in a meaningful way. There is obviously a big disconnect. Between 27-31% of the population of the US claims to attend church on a weekly basis. However, the American Church Research Project tracks real, verifiable church attendance numbers. They discovered, perhaps to the surprise of no one paying attention, that the number of people who actually attend church weekly is around half what people claim when asked.

In my state, North Carolina, the estimate of church attenders per Sunday in 2020 was just 16.7%. That was before COVID-19. I believe it. I know from investigating church attendance for a city-wide pastors' prayer group, Durham Ministers In Prayer, that in my hometown significantly less than 20% of the population were involved each week in any sort of gathering that represents the church including Sunday morning services, small groups, prayer groups, and house churches. Again, that was prior to COVID.

Since COVID studies show that attendance is only 36-60% of what it was pre-COVID. Those are existential threat numbers for many churches. With in-person attendance at an all-time low the focus now is more on engagement rather than attendance. With digital channels available on every device and podcasts replacing the desire for interpersonal interaction, people are less likely to feel a driving need to physically share the same space. Some prefer to avoid it entirely. Introverts everywhere secretly rejoice.

Now virtual gatherings are available and normative. Is that church? Is it sustainable? Even in established churches where people had close relationships before COVID, how long can those static relationships last without physically being present? How will new church relationships be developed?

It's not a perfect analogy but from my admittedly inexperienced perspective it's a little like online dating. You meet someone online and get to know them at the surface level. You can become infatuated and excited about the relationship. But to really fall in love won't you ultimately want to meet them and spend time with them in person before committing to live your lives together? Or does it all just remain in the shallow end until we become unsatisfied and move on to someone or something else? Is there a related spiritual dynamic in play with church? Should we consider the biblical analogy of Ephesians 5 comparing husbands and wives with Christ and His Church? Will God's people come together or will the exodus among Western Christians continue? We'll soon find out. For now we're in sort of a middle place waiting to see which way the pendulum swings.

Even among those who are "in church", actively participating and interacting with others, prior to COVID but especially now people are confused about what it means to be a follower of Jesus Christ in the world today. Claiming Christianity as an identifier is not the same as faithfully following Christ's commands and being actively engaged in His mission with others.

In **Matt. 16**, Jesus asked His disciples, *"Who do you say that I am?" Simon Peter answered, "You are the Christ, the Son of the living God." And Jesus said to him…upon this rock I will build My church; and the gates of Hell will not overpower it."* If Jesus were to ask today, "Who do you say I am?" He might be disappointed in some of the answers of people who claim to be His disciples.

A nationwide Barna Group survey was conducted in 2009 to determine how many Americans had a biblical worldview. 2009 seems like a lifetime ago to me. It may literally be a lifetime for some of you. Still, the results remain relevant. For the purposes of the survey, a "biblical worldview" was defined as believing these six things:

1. There is a knowable, absolute moral truth.
2. The Holy Bible contains that truth and is entirely reliable, accurate in all its principles.
3. Satan not merely a symbol; Satan is a real being that personifies and exerts evil force.
4. No one can earn their way into Heaven by being a good person or doing good things.
5. Jesus Christ is both God and man: He lived a real life on earth without sin.
6. God is the omniscient, omnipotent Creator of the world; God controls and rules the universe today.

I've already mentioned my concern about the way we live life "according to biblical principles." However, for the purposes of the research anyone who held all those beliefs was categorized as holding a biblical worldview.

The results revealed that only 9% of all American adults fall into the biblical worldview category. One subgroup of respondents was defined by those who agreed with the statement that they have made a personal to commitment to Jesus Christ that is important in their life today and that they are certain that they will go to Heaven after they die only because they confessed their sins and accepted Christ as their savior. These people were grouped in the "born-again" category.

Of that group, only 19% held all the basic views about God and the world that agree with Scripture. The confusion that I mentioned is evident. While 79% believe the Bible is accurate, only 46% believe there is absolute moral truth. Only 40% believe Satan is a real being or evil force. 53% believe we can earn our way into Heaven with good works. Only 38% strongly believe that Jesus was without sin. Yet 93% say that God is the all-powerful, all-knowing creator of the universe who still rules it today. Does any of that make sense? George Barna commented on the results.

"There are a several troubling patterns... First, although most Americans consider themselves to be Christian and say they know the content of the Bible, <u>less than one out of ten Americans demonstrate such knowledge through their actions</u>. (*underlined by the author for emphasis) Second, the generational pattern suggests that parents are not focused on guiding their children to have a biblical worldview. One of the challenges for parents, though, is that you cannot give what you do not have, and most parents do not possess such a perspective on life. That raises a third challenge, which relates to the job that Christian churches, schools, and parachurch ministries are doing in Christian education. Finally, even though a central element of being a Christian is to embrace basic biblical principles and incorporate them into one's worldview,

there has been no change in the percentage of adults or even born-again adults in the past 13 years regarding the possession of a biblical worldview. "

The bottom line – since 2009, the US population has grown by more than fifty-two million people. Yet the numbers of those who are committed to Christ and His Church are not increasing numerically or by percentage when measured against the way they live their lives by the standards of the Word of God. In fact, with the passing of each year the church is losing ground in America according to almost all verifiable measures.

Why are so many Christians confused? Why are believers failing to communicate and pass along spiritual truth to our children and others? Where is the Church of Jesus Christ in all of this? What is Church?

This is important. If the Church truly belongs to Jesus, and if He is the Light and the Hope of the world, then we need to know if what we are doing as churches is what He wants us to do; and more importantly if what kind of people we have become in our churches is what He wants us to be. We need to understand the Church that Jesus is building.

In the next chapter we're going to examine the Church in terms of history. We'll consider the following questions. What is God's relationship with humanity from the beginning until now? How is God guiding the world and how does His Church fit into His plan?

Reflections

Take some time to consider and answer these questions. If you're able, discuss this with your friends, both Christian and non, and get their perspective before you write your own conclusions.

Does the world need the Church?

_____

_____

_____

_____

What is the church primarily known for?

_____

_____

_____

_____

How does the Church fit into God's plan for the world?

_____

_____

_____

_____

_____

Chapter 5

God Has A Wonderful Plan For The Church

P eople of a certain age like me may recognize the play on words in the title of this chapter. When I was first saved in 1970 there was a little Gospel tract called, "The Four Spiritual Laws." Believe it or not, this tiny, simple booklet was mass produced and handed out to millions of people. It was left in who knows how many restaurants, restrooms, and school libraries by earnest, young Jesus People. I was among them.

My friends and I had given our lives to Jesus and we were determined to live for Him just as He died to save us from sin and death. But what did that mean? For one thing, we met together at every opportunity; at school, in churches that would have us, at public parks, in homes, at the local coffee house (*Google Christian Coffee House Movement), anywhere. We took advantage of every opportunity to tell people about Jesus.

But tell them what? The Four Spiritual Laws tract presented a clear message about God and His plan of salvation from sin and death. God always has a story and a plan. There's a reason we were saved and transformed. Somehow the Church fits into His story. Let's look and see if we can discover why God came up with the idea of the Church of Jesus Christ in the first place.

In the beginning, God created us in His image for two reasons. First, human beings are created to have relationship with God. That was His desire, as incredible as it sounds. Immortal God engaged in a loving relationship with His creation, mortal human beings.

Second, we are created in His likeness so that we can actively participate in His great plan for Creation. Yes, God really has a plan for humanity and for history. You're not here by cosmic accident. You were created by God in your mother's womb with a purpose. God wanted then, and still desires now, a holy people, a consecrated family to share His glory. That's pretty unselfish. Unfortunately, as the book of Genesis explains people became separated from God because of sin. God is righteous, just, and holy. He can't associate with sin. Despite the first humans' treasonous rebellion, God still loved His creation. Things couldn't remain the way there were. Something remarkable and divine was necessary to reconcile people to God.

God chose a tribe of people, the Jews, to carry His name, His word, and His glory. He set up a system of laws and prophets whereby He would speak to them, instruct them, and coexist with them in the Universe. Eventually that system was not satisfactory to God. He wanted more than mere coexistence. His eternal will is to have true relationship with people built on the framework of His nature of love, grace, and mercy.

To address this disconnect He initiated a plan for the redemption of mankind that would bring His only Son, Jesus, to earth. Jesus willingly came to earth for us. He lived the sinless life that we were not able to live to reverse the curse of sin and death. Then, in an amazing act of obedience to His Father and out of unfathomable love for us, Jesus bore the entire weight of our sins on a Roman instrument of torture, nailed to a cross, and died in our place. He endured the punishment that we rightly deserved and should have received for humanity's rebellion to God.

Now, for all who will receive Jesus as Lord and Savior by asking for forgiveness of their sins, turning away from rebellion, and through the voluntary surrender of human will to God's will through obedience to His commands; in His grace, God the Father grants us all the rights, privileges, and promises that are reserved for His children. He invites us to be members of His family. Through the love, grace, and mercy of Jesus Christ we can now be adopted into the family of God with all of the rights and privileges of the Firstborn. God's family is known as the *ekklēsia* in the original language of scripture, the gathering or assembly of His people. This is the Church of Jesus Christ.

"For we are the temple of the living God; just as God said," I WILL DWELL IN THEM AND WALK AMONG THEM; AND I WILL BE THEIR GOD, AND THEY SHALL BE MY PEOPLE."
II Cor. 6:16

In Christ the Church was established. Jesus declares in **Matthew 16:18**, "*I will build My church; and the gates of Hell will not prevail against it."* It is important to note that the church is not a human institution. Humans did not conceive it or establish it. The Church is not a human endeavor. It is a living organism created by God. The Church is His Body, the Body of Christ, the multiplication of Jesus on Earth that was established through His disciples, the Apostles.

According to the Gospels and the Book of Acts the Church started with twelve disciples, increased to at least 120 at Pentecost, and multiplied to 3000 later that day in Jerusalem. It quickly grew to more than 5000 men representing perhaps as many as 30,000 men, women, and children in just a few months. Later believers were driven from Jerusalem under persecution. Then the Church expanded into all of the nearby regions. It subsequently continued to spread the message of the Good News and its reach and influence continually advanced exponentially.

Eventually, the Church changed the trajectory of the heretofore mighty Roman Empire. From the time Paul and Silas were in Thessalonica and the Jews brought them before city authorities charging in **Acts 17:6**, *"These men who have upset the world have come here also,"* the Church purposely went out into all the known world, preaching the Gospel and demonstrating the Kingdom of God by the way they lived their lives, with demonstrations of the supernatural power of God occurring in the natural world.

From its inception the Church went from a weak, persecuted minority in a world-dominating, Emperor-worshipping empire, to the Emperor Constantine's conversion in 312 AD, to the Emperor Theodosius I in the year 380 AD declaring the weakened Roman Empire officially, "A Christian Empire." Interesting side note-Theodosius was baptized after his conversion by the Bishop of Thessalonica. This is the result of the faithful testimony of Paul, Silas, and those who followed from Thessalonica. It is evidence that our actions today do matter in the lives of those who will follow.

History books are full of information about the expansion of the Church in the Western world following this time. What is little known in Western History is that the Church also continued its expansion in the opposite direction making disciples and growing in influence throughout the Eastern world all the way to the Pacific coast of China.

Amazing right? Then what happened? During the first 300 years or so of its existence the Church slowly drifted away from the foundation laid by Jesus and the Apostles in the Bible. Increasing dependence on human rather than divine leadership led to the teachings of men replacing the teachings of scripture. Obedience to men soon became a demand by those in power in the church. Authority to rule was granted by believers and enforced by powerful rulers. Power corrupts. Soon politics invaded the church.

As a result, the Church in the West split from the Eastern branch and became known as the Roman Catholic Church. The Church in the East became known as the Orthodox Church. It too suffered from this shift in power from divine to human inspiration. From this and other historical examples you would think believers would have learned over time that the Church does not do well when it becomes intertwined with the State. Please don't misunderstand me. Both entities are established and ordained by God. Romans 13:1-7 makes that very clear. But Church and State serve very different purposes in God's plan for the world. They are not of equal value in God's eyes and they are incompatible as marriage partners.

The Bible carries this warning for believers. **II Cor. 6:14-18,** *"Do not be unequally yoked with unbelievers. For what partnership has righteousness with lawlessness? Or what fellowship has light with darkness? What accord has Christ with Belial? Or what portion does a believer share with an unbeliever? What agreement has the temple of God with idols? For we are the temple of the living God; as God said, "I will make my dwelling among them and walk among them, and I will be their God, and they shall be my people. Therefore go out from their midst, and be separate from them, says the Lord, and touch no unclean thing; then I will welcome you, and I will be a father to you, and you shall be sons and daughters to me, says the Lord Almighty."*

In a few short centuries the church (little "c") went from being persecuted, passionate, moral, and spiritually powerful, to being state-owned and controlled, imperial, spiritually and morally weak, corrupt. The Roman Catholic system, as it usurped the place of Christ as mediator between God and man, led the church and the world into the Dark Ages and persecuted many innocent people, including true believers. The Eastern Church fared no better during those times, compromised by strife, division, and powerful forces from within and without. By the

Middle Ages the church indeed looked dark, nearly dead, and in human terms destined only for the dusty pages of history books.

That's what it looked like even to those in the Church. However, Jesus would not let His church go down in flames or end with a pathetic whimper as we'll see in the next chapter.

Reflections

Before reading on let's do a little digging. Feel free to search online and add your own opinions.

What factors led to the corruption of the church from its beginning through the Middle Ages?

_____

_____

_____

_____

What parallels, if any, do you see in the church today?

_____

_____

_____

_____

What instructions from the Bible would help correct these negative trends?

_____

_____

_____

_____

_____

Chapter 6
The Witness of History

Easter Sunday was a big day at First Methodist Church in El Dorado, Arkansas. My family was there every Sunday and Wednesday. I sang in the choir, attended Sunday School, and was a leader in the MYF youth group. I had recently found Jesus at that stadium crusade and surrendered to Him as Lord. As a result, I was seeing everything with new eyes. The songs, the liturgy, and the symbolism of the stained-glass windows came alive to me. Now I worshiped God from my heart, in spirit and in truth.

As was the case every Easter Sunday the service was packed with people. Every seat was filled. The service was powerful and moving and then it was over. The large pipe organ had thundered the last refrain of "All Hail The Power of Jesus' Name." The benediction had been pronounced. The wooden railing around the front of the sanctuary was lined with plastic pots of white Easter lilies wrapped in purple foil tied with white ribbon. Our church had an Easter tradition of donating dozens of lilies to the residents of the town's nursing homes. As people filed out my fellow recently saved friends and I began taking lilies out the front doors and down the long stone staircase to waiting vehicles. Hands full, we walked under the large balcony where moments earlier the pews had been filled with more than 100 men, women, and children both young and old.

Suddenly, behind us there was a strange ripping sound. It started gradually then quickly turned into a forceful roar. My friends and I were in the foyer as it filled with a blinding cloud of what we assumed was smoke. Confusion and more than a little panic ensued as people hurried to get out of the way. We went outside where we could breathe and stood there stunned, not comprehending what had happened. Then we realized we were covered not in smoke but in dust. One of the ushers came out and announced that the heavy plaster ceiling under the balcony had collapsed. He organized us and we all ran back in to help anyone that may be buried under the rubble. Dust was still settling but what we could see was frightening.

The heavy wooden pews were partially flattened by the sheer weight of the plaster and steel mesh laying on top of them. People were shouting one thing or another. As shock turned into determination, we began working together lifting the interconnected heavy sheet of plaster, calling out and stopping to listen for a response from anyone that might be trapped underneath. Miraculously, even though people were still going in and out of the sanctuary at the time, no one was under the balcony when the ceiling came down. Had the collapse occurred during the service no doubt many people would have been injured. Some may not have survived.

That day I realized that God still works miracles for His people and His Church.

We ended the last chapter with the decline and seeming collapse of the Church in the Middle Ages. Things looked bad. The Church had little positive influence in the world. But once again, God was ahead of the problem. Remember, He works miracles. Just as the Lord was in the grave for three days and then rose to life, so too His Church was resurrected according to the prophecies of scripture. Consider the words of the Prophet **Isaiah 42:1-9**.

"Behold my servant, whom I uphold, my chosen, in whom my soul delights; I have put my Spirit upon him; he will bring forth justice to the nations. He will not cry aloud or lift up his voice, or make it heard in the street; a bruised reed he will not break, and a faintly burning wick he will not quench; he will faithfully bring forth justice. He will not grow faint or be discouraged till he has established justice in the earth; and the coastlands wait for his law. Thus says God, the Lord, who created the heavens and stretched them out, who spread out the earth and what comes from it, who gives breath to the people on it and spirit to those who walk in it: "I am the Lord; I have called you in righteousness; I will take you by the hand and keep you; I will give you as a covenant for the people, a light for the nations, to open the eyes that are blind, to bring out the prisoners from the dungeon, from the prison those who sit in darkness. I am the Lord; that is my name; my glory I give to no other, nor my praise to carved idols. Behold, the former things have come to pass, and new things I now declare; before they spring forth I tell you of them."

Through courageous men like John Wycliffe who translated the Bible into English, and William Tyndale who published it for the common man, God initiated the restoration and recovery of the true Church. God gave people His Word in their own language so they could read it themselves. The early Catholic reformer John Huss took up Wycliffe's cause that the church should find its authority in Scripture and not in the traditions of man. His last words (which turned out to be prophetic) as he was being tied to be burned at the stake were, *"in a hundred years, God will raise up a man whose calls for reform cannot be suppressed."*

Martin Luther nailed his Ninety-Five Theses of Contention to the church door in Wittenberg, Germany exactly 102 years later and ignited what would later became known as the Protestant Reformation.

Men like John Calvin and John Knox followed Luther, standing on the principle of "sola scriptura," meaning "only scripture," renouncing the authority of corrupt church leaders and reclaiming the authority of God through His Word, the Bible. Once again Jesus built His Church according to His standards. God made it evident through His Word that the Church is not a building, an institution, or a hierarchy commanded by men in high positions of authority that they have granted to themselves. The Church is actually the people of God, called and led by Jesus Christ Himself, walking in obedience to His commands, practicing the essentials, fulfilling the divine purpose, based on sound theology and doctrine delivered by God to people through The Holy Bible, living lives of complete surrender and submission to the sovereignty of God.

This wasn't just a return to the early Church, but a leap forward toward the victorious Church that we see foreshadowed in the Book of Revelation.

From the Reformation followed the Moravians upon whom it was said, *"the Holy Spirit fell and then the brethren learned to love one another."* They began the modern missionary movement and started a prayer meeting that went on 24/7 for over 100 years. From these missionaries, people like Jonathan Edwards, John Wesley, George Whitfield, and others were converted during what we now call "The First Great Awakening," which was characterized by outdoor preaching, apostolic church planting, and discipleship.

In the 1800's the Holiness Movement swept the world and birthed a great outpouring of Christian social activism that included people like William Wilberforce, the minister and political leader that led Great Britain to abandon and abolish the wickedness of the international slave trade.

In 1865 Hudson Taylor founded the China Inland Mission, the model of cross-cultural missions as we know it today. He was personally responsible for bringing 800 missionaries to China, founding 125

Christian schools, and leading 18,000 people to Christ. Because of his dedication and sacrifice and others who followed in his footsteps, the church in China today has known nothing but unending revival and the transformation of billions of lives. It is the largest and fastest growing church movement on earth today in spite of monumental oppression.

In the late 1800's and early 1900's, God used the Welsh and Azusa St. revivals to restore the transformative power and the spiritual gifts bestowed by the Holy Spirit to the Church. The Pentecostal movement accelerated this restoration across the entire world. My own life and work today and the witness of many others is a direct result of what God did in the 1960's and 70's through the Charismatic Renewal. The songs of scripture and praise from those days now ring through churches around the world and across denominations along with the hymns of earlier ages.

We can see that beginning with the early church, through the reformers at the end of the Dark Ages, and proceeding on to today, God has been not only restoring everything that was lost from the failure and collapse of the church, but rather He has always been launching His Church forward toward its ultimate destiny. In the midst of today's chaotic and dangerous world the Church of Jesus Christ continues to influence people, tribes, nations, governments, and entire societies toward the Gospel. Meanwhile, Satan and his world forces of darkness continually oppose Jesus and resist His Church. Their war against God and His people is evident in the ascendancy of human secularism, the syncretism of world religions and spirituality, the threat of world domination by radical Islam, and the demise of faithful Christianity in places that are Hell-bent toward everything but God.

Yet we are often reminded in the Bible to fear no evil, for the Lord is with us. I believe we are at a moment of serious inflection as humans, as believers, and in the Church. We are moving toward the summation of all things in Jesus Christ. The time prophetically announced in **Ephesians 4:11-16** is coming soon.

"And He gave some as apostles, and some as prophets, and some as evangelists, and some as pastors and teachers, for the equipping of the saints for the work of service, to the building up of the body of Christ; until we all attain to the unity of the faith, and of the knowledge of the Son of God, to a mature man, to the measure of the stature which belongs to the fullness of Christ. As a result, we are no longer to be children, tossed here and there by waves and carried about by every wind of doctrine, by the trickery of men, by craftiness in deceitful scheming; but speaking the truth in love, we are to grow up in all aspects into Him who is the head, even Christ, from whom the whole body, being fitted and held together by what every joint supplies, according to the proper working of each individual part, causes the growth of the body for the building up of itself in love."

The fulfillment of this prophecy of scripture is rapidly approaching when every faithful Christian will move together in the love of God and the power of the Holy Spirit. Every true believer will be equipped and engaged in the work of the ministry, serving God faithfully and effectively with Christ as the Head of His Church. But as we examine the state of the church today we can see that God is going to have to do something major, something powerful, something *awesome*, to bring that about. I want to ask you, are you committed to God's plan, to His will? Because He's committed to you, if you believe in Jesus and are truly engaged in His Body, His Church.

It has been said that not all who are in the church are of the Church. Only Jesus knows. He challenges His followers to understand what is happening around them and to examine and be aware of our situation. **Matthew 16:3**, *"You know how to interpret the appearance of the sky, but you cannot interpret the signs of the times."* It is important that we consider where the Church is today, how we are connected in comparison to the Word of God, and to assess where we stand individually and corporately.

As an adult I came into possession of my great-grandfather's Bible. It was huge and fascinating. On those yellowed and dog-eared pages, I not only could read some of the family history captured in time, I could also see from the well-worn pages the faithfulness of my forebearers. Before, I lived my life completely unaware of the faithful Christians that had gone before me and no doubt prayed for me before I was even born. That Bible gave me a sense of connectedness and belonging that I had not known before. I have since passed it along to my niece and her children so they too will understand their lineage in the family of God.

What is your heritage? How did you come to faith and who else was involved? Who is your spiritual family? Maybe like me you don't really know or haven't given it much thought. At the end of this chapter, I am going to encourage you to read and study **Ephesians 2**. To give you a preview, look at what it says in **verses 19-22**, *"So then you are no longer strangers and aliens, but you are fellow citizens with the saints, and are of God's household, having been built on the foundation of the apostles and prophets, Christ Jesus Himself being the corner stone, in whom the whole building, being fitted together, is growing into a holy temple in the Lord, in whom you also are being built together into a dwelling of God in the Spirit."*

This is God's description of the Church of Jesus Christ and who you are as one of His saints. That's not even the best part, but you'll have to wait until later in the book to read about the Victorious Church.

Let's finish this chapter by reading **Psalm 2.** *"Why do the nations rage and the peoples plot in vain? The kings of the earth set themselves, and the rulers take counsel together, against the Lord and against his Anointed, saying, "Let us burst their bonds apart and cast away their cords from us." He who sits in the heavens laughs; the Lord holds them in derision. Then he will speak to them in his wrath, and terrify them in his fury, saying, "As for me, I have set my King on Zion, my holy hill." I will tell of the decree: The Lord said to me, "You are my Son; today I have begotten you. Ask of me, and I will make the nations your heritage, and the ends of the earth your possession. You shall break them with a rod of iron and dash them in pieces like a potter's* *vessel." Now therefore, O kings, be wise, be warned, O rulers of the earth. Serve the Lord with fear and rejoice with trembling. Kiss the Son, lest he be angry, and you perish in the way, for his wrath is quickly kindled. Blessed are all who take refuge in him.*

Can you see yourself in God's family today? What is Church? This is Church. A lot of people are praying today for revival and awakening. From time-to-time little drops of blessing from Heaven occur in a town, a nation, a people group. We see small outbreaks of people being saved, baptized, and engaging with Jesus and His mission. When this happens in your sphere of influence, among your people, where will these new believers turn for community, fellowship, and guidance? What do you make of Christ's command to make disciples of all nations? Is the church ready for that?

I'm concerned because of my own salvation story. As you've read, I was raised Methodist. I officially "joined the church" when I was 12. However, I was still lost as an Easter egg. I gave my life to Jesus Christ in 1970. As I sat in the stands of the stadium that night, I heard about sin separating people from God. For the first time I knew that was me. I felt the separation and it broke me. I asked Jesus to save me and forgive me, and He did. I had never felt so alive and clean. Amazingly so did many of my friends. It wasn't just an emotional experience. It was supernatural. God did that.

It didn't end that night. In fact, the fire of conviction leading to salvation that God started soon spread to our entire town. Almost everyone I knew turned to Jesus and we determined to live our lives for Him. Now here's the part the concerns me. The churches didn't respond well. They didn't like these "Jesus freaks" that were invading their sanctuaries and meetings. We had long hair, strange clothes, new Jesus music, and none of the religious social inhibitions that were customary. Instead of "the right hand of fellowship" as they used to say they gave us the left foot of exile right out the door.

With no place to gather and very few mature Christians willing to make disciples of us the foundation was laid for more division in the Church. Before long charismatic churches began to appear, meeting in homes and loaned or rented spaces. Unfortunately, with little maturity, sound doctrine, loving fellowship, or instruction in righteousness things often got weird and sometimes downright abusive. Some of those charismatic gatherings did survive as churches, grow into Christian maturity, and continue to do their job of making faithful disciples. But more crashed and burned taking down a multitude of people that were left hurt, abandoned, mistreated, confused, and derided. Some were terribly wounded and left feeling alone and confused to the point of rejecting not just the church, but also their faith in Jesus.

It is still happening in all types of churches. Today the spiritually walking wounded are all around us. How do we help someone with that experience? How do we avoid repeating the same mistakes in present and future moves of God?

I'm writing this book out of concern not only for the people of the last movement, but primarily for the generations that have followed. Gen X, Millennials, Gen Z, and Gen Alpha concern me the most as the trail leading to Jesus and His Church grows ever colder with the passage of time. What's the answer to this situation? Followers of Jesus must be concerned enough to ensure that the church is actually "The Church" as Christ intended. We may recognize when church is not working as it should or when it turns toxic and abusive. But how do we recognize the authentic Church and how do we engage?

In the next two chapters we'll examine what Church is in essence. Before we do, take a few moments to write down your thoughts about the basic elements that define the Church of Jesus Christ.

Reflections

What do you believe are the essentials of Church?

_____

_____

_____

_____

_____

_____

_____

_____

What are the requirements for Church according to Jesus in His Word?

_____

_____

_____

_____

_____

_____

_____

_____

_____

Chapter 7
Expectations

nother true confession. Yes, I was one of "those" pastors. I loved to experiment with different ways of doing things. My intention was to help people stretch their faith and connect with God and one another outside of church norms. Honestly, as much as I'd like to believe that's true, I'm not sure that was always my entire motivation. At heart I'm one of those odd people that actually likes change. That inclination often puts me in the minority. As a leader with the ability to effect change it can be downright disconcerting to most normal people who like things just as they have always been, thank you very much.

Our sanctuary has chairs in rows instead of pews. The platform is in front and we sit theater style. One Sunday I rearranged the chairs in the sanctuary into large semi-circles on opposite sides of the room. There was enough open space in the middle of the room for people to gather in small numbers and move around. The open area contained tables with the elements of the Lord's Supper prepared. As people came into the Sanctuary they were instantly confronted with a new challenge, what is this and where do I/we sit? All the usual rows and familiar guides were missing. The worship team was noticeably absent altogether. No explanation or instructions were provided. People were either confused or bemused, curious or irritated. Everyone walked in and had to figure it out. Some chose a spot and sat down while others stood and talked to one another at the outer ring unable to determine what to do. It made for an unusual opening.

At the appropriate time I asked everyone to please find a place and sit. A few minutes of mild chaos ensued. "Do we keep the chairs together?" Some made spaces between individuals and families. One or two dragged chairs out to sit along the walls. Once everyone had somewhat settled, I called the assembly together and stated the obvious. "Welcome. We're going to worship God differently today." After an opening prayer invoking God's presence and asking for His guidance I told everyone that we would begin by silently "singing," *I Love You Lord.* (Laurie Adams-Klein ©1978 House of Mercy Music) I explained we would mouth the words together without instruments or making any sound. Someone asked was I kidding? I assured them I was not. Hesitantly we began.

It was awkward. As we "sang" people reacted in different ways. Some looked around at others and worked together to stay on the same words at the same time. Others closed their eyes and bowed their heads, either mouthing the words or not. Some crossed their arms, stared straight ahead, and refused to participate. Some lifted their heads upward with open eyes and mouthed the words as if directly to their Creator. Around the second time through a few began to softly weep. At the end we all sat quietly for a few seconds and no one spoke or moved.

Slowly and quietly I addressed everyone. "If you were gathering with believers in some parts of China, Saudi Arabia, Pakistan, Indonesia, or Afghanistan this might be the way you had to worship together this morning: silently, secretly, so no one would hear you, report you, arrest you, bomb you, or burn down the place where you are meeting."

"Does this setup feel strange to you?" I asked. "Were you upset, either by the seating, the style of worship, no words on the screen or in your hand, having to look at other people's faces instead of the back of their heads, or something else? Is a song without sound worship? Is this church? What is Church?"

The answer to most people looking in from the outside is that church is a building where Christians hold meetings. While Christians are usually able to get beyond the building analogy and explain that people are the "real" church there still is a strong association with the facility. When asked, "Where do you go to church?" we normally respond with the name and location rather than explaining we don't "go to church," we are the church. It's a reasonable understanding that has held up for more than a century. However, the Covid-19 pandemic may have changed that forever. Maybe God intended it that way.

Historically for most Christians in free societies the church most often has taken on the form of an institution, an established and organized society with its own building, or perhaps meeting in leased or rented space. It may operate much like any other institution except for the content of the meetings. But it doesn't always look that way. We've recently learned what church is like under pandemic restrictions. Turns out the building wasn't indispensable after all except maybe as a broadcast location for the pastor and worship team. Even that paradigm doesn't always hold up. Groups meet online over podcasts and explore things like VR/MMO Church. This presents us with the opportunity to reevaluate the formation and practice of church.

As indoor meeting and masking restrictions lifted believers either couldn't wait to get back to in-person meetings in a building or are content to continue to participate as an observer in our PJs from the relative safety and comfort of our homes. Some have given up on the idea of community altogether, listening to podcasts and perhaps interacting with others about spiritual matters solely via social media. Even then people most often still identify and associate with a church that meets somewhere physical, but that too is slowly evolving. What does the future hold? I'm confident Jesus knows.

What would church look like with the loss of the gathering space or the loss of the leaders? What does it look like if the freedom to assemble goes away entirely? Those are not imaginary situations for many Christians around the world. That is the reality. Certainly then, the essence of Church is not a physical building. If not that, then what?

Is it people that are bound together in a common cause? Is church dependent on a shared sense of vision and purpose espoused by a leader or leaders?

Instead of resting on what we think we know and have experienced previously, let's see what the Bible tells us about the foundation stones of Church.

Reflections

What are your church preferences?

_____

_____

_____

_____

_____

_____

_____

_____

What do you expect when church happens?

_____

_____

_____

_____

_____

_____

_____

_____

_____

Chapter 8
The Essentials

G rowing up in church I thought I knew what it was all about. Then I unexpectedly met Jesus outside the church. He changed my life and my understanding of His Church. What I had been confident in was suddenly challenged and my experience with church expanded. I had friends from all sorts of religious and non-religious backgrounds. Suddenly we had Jesus in common and we had to find our own way of meeting, sharing our faith together, and expressing our thanks and worship to our King. We visited each other's churches. It was not always a satisfying experience. In some we were welcomed. In some we were rejected and invited to leave. Often, we were ignored and not invited to participate or return. That didn't stop us from gathering for Bible study, prayer, hanging out, sharing meals, and going out to do evangelism together.

Fortunately, we had some older saints that were willing to engage with us. They answered our questions, gently guided us when we were off base, encouraged us in our faith, and ministered to us when we were confused and hurting. This mostly happened in private homes although sometimes at odd hours in church buildings or at the lake. I still remember them fondly and hold them in high esteem as God's chosen volunteers and spiritual guides. That was where my initial reevaluation and education regarding church started. It's been a lifelong interest for me for many reasons, some of them theological and some of them much more practical. What is Church?

To clarify our understanding, we will examine Church in terms of essence, function, and form. In this chapter we'll examine the first of the three. What is the essence of the Church? By that I mean, what are the minimum essentials that are necessary for the existence of the Church?

Jesus told stories and used examples in His teaching that people could easily relate with. Often, they were agrarian or work-related comparisons that His original followers would find familiar. For an Arkansan I am not much of a farmer. But I have certainly done more than my fair share of fishing. As some of the original disciples were fishermen, it is helpful to me to compare Church with fishing. Even if you've never fished and have no practical understanding or interest in fishing personally, hang in there with me. I'll try to make it make sense.

The essence of fishing is whatever minimum essentials are necessary to achieve fishing. You may be far removed from the actual act of fishing in real life, but I'd be willing to bet that you still have a pretty good idea of what fishing entails and what components are necessary. The morning of the particular church social experiment I described in the last chapter I asked people in our congregation, what do you think are the bare minimum elements necessary for fishing? I received a wide range of answers. Before you read any further, stop and think about your own answer to this question.

Q: What things do you believe are absolutely essential for fishing?

Here are some of the answers I received from our congregation. Water, a rod & reel, a lure or other bait, a hook and line, a spear, a net, a gun, dynamite, drain the pond. Some people have a vivid thought life! However, in the end I believe these entertaining suggestions all missed on establishing the real essentials. From my viewpoint there are only two things that are absolutely necessary for fishing.

A: A person and a fish. That's it.

Point of consideration: The <u>essence</u> never changes. No matter the location, the century, the society, the people involved, or any other consideration these requirements do not vary.

Next is the <u>function</u>. The function is the purpose of fishing. The purpose of fishing is to catch fish. Other outcomes may also be in play. The act of fishing may be enjoyable or not. It may get you out of the house, expose you to nature, allow you to get a suntan, teach you patience, give you the satisfaction of achievement, or any number of other things. But other activities could also accomplish any of these goals. They are not the function of fishing. The function of fishing is to catch fish. It is the same every time. Like essence, function never changes.

<u>Form</u> on the other hand can be incredibly varied. As long the form allows for the fulfillment of the essence (a person and a fish) and fulfills the function (to catch fish) it is by definition, fishing. Form explains many of the answers from our congregation and perhaps some of the things you thought of as well. Unlike essence and function, form can change and be incredibly varied if it meets the essence and fulfills the function.

As an aside, I do recommend making sure the form you choose for fishing is legal. Dynamite might be an effective method to catch fish (perhaps as they fall from the sky) but it also carries a lot of potentially negative consequences including arrest and prosecution. Church forms should conform to legality as well unless compliance demands the violation of God's commands.

How do we determine the essence of church? As I indicated earlier, we'll use the Bible as our authority. Why? Why should we trust the Bible as opposed to another source or our own ideas? Why is it different than any other book? Here are five good reasons:

1. The Bible is an amazingly accurate record of fulfilled prophecy. God says something and it happens.
2. Despite the grand scope of a collection of books written by authors from various cultures gathered over thousands of years, it maintains a consistent theme.
3. The Bible has endured challenges for centuries.
4. The Bible's truths are confirmed by archaeology, history, and science.
5. The Human Witness-God has used the Bible to transform countless millions of lives throughout time and across all cultures.

The Bible really is the Word of God. We can trust it. Now, according to the Bible what are the minimum essentials of Church? As with the question I asked about the essence of fishing people have a lot of thoughts and ideas that may not be accurate. Let's start with the most essential element.

The Centrality of Jesus Christ

First and foremost, church, the authentic, the one and only Church in God's sight and in the Bible, is founded and built on the centrality of Jesus Christ. *"I will build My church and the gates of Hades will not prevail against it." Jesus Christ,* **Matt. 16:18**

Again, the word that we know as "Church" is the New Testament Koine Greek word, Ekklēsia. The intended meaning is the gathering of those who are specifically called. This word Ekklēsia (church) applies to gatherings of citizens summoned by an authority for a specific purpose. It wasn't a new or unfamiliar word to people in the time of Christ. The term was in common use in the city-states of ancient Greece several hundred years prior to Jesus. More on that in a minute.

Today, in our own language there are non-Christian entities that use the name "church." Some are pretty dark and I don't recommend you do a Google search, although now some of you undoubtedly will. My apologies for bringing it up. Seriously, take my word for it, save your conscience and don't do it.

There are still secular assemblies where people are called or summoned to gather by an authority for a specific purpose. Two words come to mind. Jury duty. No one who has ever been summoned for jury duty would confuse that experience with church.

Gathering with other like-minded people for a common purpose in and of itself is not the essence of church. The essence is determined by the authority that calls or summons people to the gathering. Jesus declared, *"I will build My church."* Jesus is essential to church. **Col. 1:18**. *"And He (the Lord Jesus Christ) is the head of the body, the church."*

What else is essential for Church? People. **Matthew 18:20**, *"For where two or three are gathered in my name, there am I among them."* So then, as the essence of fishing is a person and a fish, the essence of the Church is Jesus and at least two people that gather in His name. Any people? All people? As the Head of the Church Jesus is the authority that calls or summons people to gather in His name. Therefore, He is the Convener of the Church. Does the Bible tell us anything else that Jesus requires as essential? What kind of people are summoned?

Prior to the time of Christ in ancient Greece, the Ekklēsia consisted of male citizens eighteen years of age or over. They met to vote on policy, hear appeals, elect representatives, and confer special privileges on individuals at both regular meetings and special sessions. Perhaps you can still see echoes of Greek philosophy in some church meetings and practices today. It is important to note that under the Roman Empire the Greek Ekklēsia system was trampled by imperialism. Perhaps that is one reason people under Roman rule found Jesus and the Church He was building attractive. As has often been said, everyone is equal at the foot of the cross.

Jesus calls everyone, men, women, and children into the Kingdom of God and appoints them a place in His Church (Ekklēsia). All believers are called to engage and participate. **Eph. 2:19-21**, *"So then you are no longer strangers and aliens, but you are fellow citizens with the saints and members of the household of God, built on the foundation of the apostles and prophets, Christ Jesus himself being the cornerstone, in whom the whole structure, being joined together, grows into a holy temple in the Lord."*

Jesus Himself not only calls and puts forth the essential qualifications for people to engage in His Church, He also provides individuals with the necessary standing before God to meet His qualifications. Following are the qualifications for citizenship in the Kingdom of God. Jesus issues the summons to join the gathering of the Church according to these criteria.

Personal Faith in Jesus Christ as Savior and Lord

Essential faith isn't just a belief that Jesus is Messiah/God/Savior of humankind. **James 2:19**, *"You believe that God is one. You do well; the demons also believe, and shudder."* There aren't supposed to be demons in the church, although some might argue they exist based on personal experience. If there are demons in the church they are not authorized by Jesus and are therefore illegitimate. Let's cast them out together in His Name. Again, I digress. I'll try and restrain myself. Back to the matter at hand.

What kind of faith is truly essential faith? **John 3:3**, *Jesus answered and said to him, "Truly, truly, I say to you, unless one is born again he cannot see the kingdom of God."* Those called by Jesus to His Church are new creations in Christ. They have recognized and been convicted of their sin before Holy God. They have asked God for forgiveness in Jesus' name. They have repented, meaning they have renounced sin and determined to turn away from rebellion to God and walk toward Him. They have surrendered to Jesus Christ as King and Lord. They have been born again by the Spirit of God. They are not the same people they were before their encounter with Jesus and surrender to His Lordship. They are new. They are clean and God counts them as His holy family.

Not only that, genuine, saving faith is not a one-time decision that causes a momentary change in behavior that disappears over time. Essential faith is demonstrated through consistent action in agreement with God's revealed will. **James 2:20** – *"But are you willing to recognize, you foolish fellow, that faith without works is useless?"* Our good deeds do not save us or make us fit for the Church and ultimately Heaven. Mere belief that Jesus is God and declaring it is true is not essential faith in itself. When we have personal faith in Jesus Christ that transforms us and makes a living member of the Church, confirming evidence will be evident in our lives.

Now, per this analogy if a jury is made up of twelve people, how many constitute a church? What does the Bible say?

At Least Two or More People Sharing Faith

One person and some alone time Jesus is wonderful, but it is not Church. This truth carries major implications in our current situation with livestreams, podcasts, VR and other yet to be developed technological and social advances. Does this mean people <u>of</u> the Church must gather in person with others to <u>be</u> the Church? That's a very good question. Let's focus on what the Bible does and does not say.

Matt. 18:19-20, *"Again I say to you, that if two of you agree on earth about anything that they may ask, it shall be done for them by My Father who is in heaven. For where two or three have gathered together in My name, I am there in their midst."*

I Peter 2:5 – *"you also, as living stones, are being built up as a spiritual house for a holy priesthood, to offer up spiritual sacrifices acceptable to God through Jesus Christ."*

I Cor. 12:12-13 – *"For even as the body is one and yet has many members, and all the members of the body, though they are many, are one body, so also is Christ. For by one Spirit we were all baptized into one body, whether Jews or Greeks, whether slaves or free, and we were all made to drink of one Spirit."*

From these passages we can see that God is invested in community, spiritual family. In one sense you could say that His relationship with us is virtual, in that we are not physically in His presence. Or are we?

"Where shall I go from your Spirit? Or where shall I flee from your presence? If I ascend to heaven, you are there! If I make my bed in Sheol, you are there! If I take the wings of the morning and dwell in the uttermost parts of the sea, even there your hand shall lead me, and your right hand shall hold me." **Psalm 139:7-10**

We may not experience God with our five human senses, but does that mean He is not physically present with us when we meet as His Church? It appears that He is in fact physically present. Jesus seems pretty invested in being physically present with His disciples. He came in physical form to save us. He appeared in a different physical form after His resurrection. He ascended into Heaven in physical form. He promised to return in physical form. The marriage supper of the Lamb certainly indicates His, and our, physical presence. Jesus is very invested in His Church meeting together physically. In fact, there is the clear encouragement of scripture to meet together as His Church in **Heb. 10:24-25**. *"And let us consider how to stir up one another to love and good works, not neglecting to meet together, as is the habit of some, but encouraging one another, and all the more as you see the Day drawing near."*

In summary, the Church is made up of Jesus and more than one person with personal faith in Him. God declares the Church a body with multiple members, a spiritual house where God dwells with His people. And what is the relationship of these people? How does Jesus expect them to relate and function?

A Commitment to Jesus Christ and to Each Other

This is where churches often break down and go astray from the teachings of the Bible. Let's take a deeper look.

Commitment to Jesus as Lord. **John 3:36**, *"He who believes in the Son has eternal life; but he who does not obey the Son will not see life, but the wrath of God abides on him."* **John 14:15**, *"If you love Me, you will keep My commandments."*

Commitment to each other as members of Jesus' Church family. **Eph. 2:19-22**, *"So then you are no longer strangers and aliens, but you are fellow citizens with the saints, and are of God's household, having been built on the foundation of the apostles and prophets, Christ Jesus Himself being the corner stone, in whom the whole building, being fitted together, is growing into a holy temple in the Lord, in whom you also are being built together into a dwelling of God in the Spirit."* **I Cor. 12:24-27**, *"But God has so composed the body, giving more abundant honor to that member which lacked, so that there may be no division in the body, but that the members may have the same care for one another. And if one member suffers, all the members suffer with it; if one member is honored, all the members rejoice with it. Now you are Christ's body, and individually members of it."* **Hebrews 10:23-25**, *"Let us hold fast the confession of our hope without wavering, for He who promised is faithful; and let us consider how to stimulate one another to love and good deeds, not forsaking our own assembling together, as is the habit of some, but encouraging one another; and all the more as you see the day drawing near."*

Commitment to one another requires us to follow God's commands, particularly in the way we treat our brothers and sisters in Christ. We are instructed to:

- Serve one another.
- Accept one another.
- Forgive one another.

- Greet one another.
- Bear one another's burdens.
- Be devoted to one another in love.
- Honor one another.
- Teach one another.
- Submit to one another.
- Encourage one another.

How are we doing with the "one another's" in our churches? I have a dear friend that we'll call Natalya. She was born and grew up in a country that heavily and violently persecutes Christians. Natalya came to faith in Jesus as a young adult through the loving influence of a few courageous expat Christian workers. Shortly after conversion her family rejected her and demanded she renounce Jesus. When she refused, her newfound faith and witness brought her into conflict not only with her family but also with the government. It was a very dangerous time for Natalya. She was forced to flee the country alone in fear for her life. She has lived in the West for more than two decades, separated from her family with no way home. She's still praying and seeking a way to return because she loves her family, her people, and her nation.

Our church was called by God in 1997 to commit to getting the Gospel to her people. Since then, we have shared in a great deal of ministry and relationship with this remarkable woman. Recently Natalya recalled for us her first meeting with our church family with joy and weeping. She recounted as a newly relocated believer how for the first time since her forced exile she experienced the kindness and hospitality she was accustomed to among her own people, in her home country, as she met and worshiped with us. For the first time in exile in the Western world she felt loved, embraced, accepted, valued, connected to God and to His Church. All of us felt that same connectedness as she shared her experiences. She ministered to us. It was a deeply spiritual and moving meeting as if the Kingdom of God had come to earth. If you will allow, according to scripture, it did.

This is evidence of the Church in the world, the body of Christ, the family of God, the spiritual building where the Spirit of God dwells. That's the essence of Church. Jesus meeting with His people. It's not a feeling although feelings may happen. Church is the evidence of faith in Jesus as Savior and Lord. It's the evidence of things unseen. That kind of faith, that kind of gathering of God's people is not about us. The evidence of faith occurs whenever and wherever Jesus is building His Church.

Jesus says in **John 4:24**, *"God is spirit, and those who worship him must worship in spirit and truth."* We didn't sing songs in Natalya's language. We didn't adopt her dress or culture and she didn't adopt ours. We didn't meet in secret as she had in her home country. Church that morning didn't have anything to do with our location, our liturgy, our cultural norms and standards, or anything else. We simply focused on the essentials, Jesus and a few of His followers met together and worshiped Him. He does the rest.

We need to always value and protect the essence of Church. The form may change to meet the need of the moment, but the essence never changes.

Reflections

Briefly outline the essence of the Church in a way that you will remember it. Keep this in mind as you read the rest of the book, and as you live your life.

Chapter 9
Selah

In the next chapter we're going to begin examining the function of the Church, its purpose. Before we do there's a little instruction in the Bible that you may find helpful. In the Psalms you will often see the Hebrew word, "Selah." This word, this instruction, is translated several different ways in English and other languages depending on the version you are reading. In context one way to translate it is, *Selah-to pause to think about what the Scripture says; to reflect on the meaning of what has been spoken or read before continuing.* That's what we're going to do here. Before we examine the function of the Church this is a good time to pause and consider what you've read so far, including something that Jesus said after His resurrection.

> **John 20:21-22**, *"So Jesus said to them again, "Peace be with you; as the Father has sent Me, I also send you." And when He had said this, He breathed on them and said to them, "Receive the Holy Spirit."*

Think about that and all it means for you regarding the Church and your place in it. Today for some reason it is all too common in our churches to diminish the person and the work of the Holy Spirit. But you really can't have Church without the Holy Spirit.

I don't know where you stand with God at this moment. Perhaps you made a commitment to Jesus some time ago and remain firm in your faith. Maybe you feel good and confident about that. If that's you this pause will be refreshing.

Maybe you made a commitment in faith at one time, but you feel you have lost some of that initial zeal. Perhaps your commitment to God has come loose and frayed a little over time and now you feel shaky in your faith and relationship with Jesus. If that's you this pause is a good time to remember and reflect on where your faith began and to see where you stand right now.

You may have been born into a family that claimed Christian faith as a heritage, a cultural identity, but you've never really had a transformative encounter with the living God. You wonder if this Jesus thing is real? You can use this pause to review how you feel about that now. Perhaps you can speak to Jesus about it. He's listening and paying attention.

You may be of another faith, agnostic, or atheist and are reading this book out of curiosity. If so, I am going to assume that you are searching for truth. This pause is a good time to search your heart and see how secure you are in your own beliefs. Whatever your situation I'm honored to encounter you on your own spiritual journey.

I want to offer this pause as an invitation to you. If in the course of this book you have felt something stirring inside you that makes you desire a deeper encounter with God the Creator and Sustainer, there is one sure way to find what you're looking for. Jesus said something profound to a young man that was also seeking truth. His words are recorded in the Bible in **John 14:6**. *"Jesus said to him, "I am the way, and the truth, and the life. No one comes to the Father except through me."*

That's either the truth or Jesus is not who He says He is. However, if it is true then the rest of His claims, statements, actions, and intentions are worth serious consideration.

Wherever you are on your path through life, truth, and faith I encourage you to consider this statement. In this simple declaration is a profound power that has changed the life and direction of millions of people since Jesus walked the earth. If you want to meet and follow Jesus, just ask Him to guide you. People often tell me, *"I don't know how to pray."* It is really not as hard as we imagine or as some people claim it is. Jesus is very approachable. He is not dead. He is very much alive. He is with you right now. He is totally invested in starting and cultivating a relationship with you that will literally save your life and give you a divine purpose. Jesus' pledge of commitment to you is recorded in **John 3:16-17.** *"For God so loved the world (*that includes you), that he gave his only Son, that whoever believes in him should not perish but have eternal life. For God did not send his Son into the world to condemn the world, but in order that the world might be saved through him."*

If you'd like to pledge your commitment to Him in response, simply talk with Him. That's prayer and yes, it takes faith. You can tell Jesus you believe He is God and you trust Him to lead and guide you. You can ask Jesus to forgive your sins and make you completely clean of every bad thing and every bad thought you've had before God. I and millions of other people will tell you; He truly will change you and your life from the inside out. Jesus promises when you do that, you'll really know God and He will always be with you.

If you are secure in your faith and concerned about church and where you fit in, I encourage you to ask Jesus for wisdom and direction and begin to express and practice your commitment to the essentials of Church. He promises He will send the Holy Spirit to help, guide, and lead you.

"But when he, the Spirit of truth, comes, he will guide you into all the truth. He will not speak on his own; he will speak only what he hears, and he will tell you what is yet to come." **John 16:13 NIV**

Whatever you decide, however you are moved or not moved, please take time right now to make a conscious determination to consider Jesus and respond to His invitation with purpose. We make so many auto-matic, unconscious decisions that have a great impact on us, our present, our future, and on the people around us. Please don't allow this choice to be one of them. Be mindful in the way that God intended when He fashioned you in your mother's womb, breathed life into you, gave you a sound mind, and brought you to this moment in time. Please, pause and think on these things and then, act on what you believe.

In the next chapter we'll look at the reasons Jesus created the Church. We'll see His purposes being worked out as He builds His Church here on Earth. For now…

Selah.

Chapter 10
Function

P reviously we've learned that Church is:

1. Not a physical place or building
2. Not a human idea or organization
3. Not headed by human beings

We've also explored the essence of Church – Jesus and at least two people he has called together sharing faith. But why Church in the first place? What is the Church to accomplish? How is it supposed to work?

Many people are asking these questions, believers and skeptics alike. With 2000+ years of history under the Church's belt there have been a lot of good things accomplished by churches in the name of God, and unfortunately a lot of bad things have also occurred. How could that happen?

After I was saved at 15, I lived enthusiastically for Jesus the entirety of my High School career. I had a large group of Christian friends that were likewise "on fire" for God. Day by day we gathered for Bible study, prayer, snacks, games, activities, and sharing our faith publicly. Some of us were musically inclined and we formed a band and called ourselves Sunday's Children. It was a large group that today would be known as a musical collective. We played primarily at Christian coffee houses, outdoor concerts, pizza parlors, flatbed trucks in shopping center parking lots, and any other space that would have us. We traveled and toured around the Ark-La-Tex (yes, that's a thing) playing for churches, youth camps, and retreats. We put together our own evangelistic crusades with other bands and speakers that could relate to young people.

Wherever we went, church happened. Our songs were mostly originals with some popular Jesus Music interspersed in the sets. We'd always stop and preach the Good News and offer the opportunity for salvation in Jesus. We prayed for and with a lot of people and sure enough, God would show up. We witnessed hundreds giving their lives to Jesus. Occasionally someone would get healed of a disease or injury. We saw crazy manifestations of God's presence. One night we watched a cloud in the shape of a perfect cross pass slowly in front of a full moon in an otherwise cloudless sky and we felt a sense of awe and peace.

Honestly it was the most special time in our lives and the life of our community. Only later did we learn that the same thing was happening in other places all over the nation. Everything we experienced with Jesus was outside of what we had previously known and considered normal. We expected Jesus to return at any minute and we lived our lives with that in mind.

The summer after my senior year our band supported the First Baptist Church youth group on a tour of the Northeast USA. We played on the streets of Harlem in NYC while sharing Jesus door to door. The cops thought we were crazy. We played and performed in churches and on town squares in New York, Massachusetts, Connecticut, Rhode Island, and Pennsylvania. Then it was over. I ended the tour by flying home and moving to begin my freshman year at Centenary College in Shreveport, LA.

I expected to find the same community there, but it didn't happen. I visited the Methodist Student Movement meeting and was introduced to the film, "A Clockwork Orange." Not exactly encouraging in my Christian walk. I tried the Baptist Student Ministry, but they didn't understand what I was seeking. Then I ran into some charismatic Christians. They seemed like the people I had done Lay Witness Missions within the Methodist Church. Charismatic was a new term to me. However, they seemed very enthusiastic and happy to welcome me to their group. In fact, shortly after I started attending their meetings, they told me they thought I should be in leadership. They followed that announcement with the revelation that there was a problem. They said unless I was baptized in the Holy Spirit and spoke in tongues, I wasn't really a Christian.

That shocked me. Based on the experiences I'd had and my own personal interactions with Jesus I was pretty sure I was saved. Still, it troubled me. I knew there was a Holy Spirit. The Methodist Church had the cross and the flame symbol representing the Holy Spirit. I'd grown up with that, but I didn't know much else. I didn't know what it meant to be baptized in the Holy Spirit. Turns out they meant I had to speak in tongues as evidence that I was saved, or my salvation wasn't genuine.

I was deeply troubled. Remember, I'd been on a mission for God for three years. I loved Jesus and had committed to serve Him with my whole heart and my whole life. If I had missed a step for salvation, I wanted to correct it. They tried to lay hands on me and pray for me. Nope. That was weird to me, and I didn't want to be influenced to do something just to please them. If Jesus wanted me to get baptized in the Holy Spirit and speak in tongues, He'd have to make it happen without their involvement. So, I came up with a plan. I'd go off by myself and pray until something happened. And that's exactly what I did.

I went to the attic of the Science Building where I knew I could be alone. It was at night on a weekend, and no one was around. I began to labor in prayer, begging for Jesus to show me the way. This went on for a while. Finally, I said a few syllables out loud that didn't make sense to me. Immediately I began to question where that came from. Was it God or was it me? I didn't understand what I'd said. I felt foolish. I decided I was making it up in my mind and I shut it down. I cried. Then, I got angry.

I was angry with myself for caring what these people thought about me and my salvation. I was angry with God for making this so difficult and confusing. I felt tricked by God for letting me believe I was saved all those years. And that's where my mind and my heart changed again, this time not for good. I was angry that I had served Him and led so many people to make the same decision I had made if it wasn't really true. Mostly I felt betrayed and alone. All my friends were gone. I decided I wouldn't be fooled again.

I told God that night that I wanted Him to leave me alone and I'd do the same to Him. I still believed God existed and that Jesus was the only way to God. There was too much water under the bridge, too much evidence to deny it was truth. But I didn't want to serve God anymore and I certainly didn't want anything more to do with those charismatics. Or the Methodists, or the Baptists. The big, beautiful Church without divisions that I had known with all my high school friends and our mentors was long gone. For the first time since I had become a follower of Jesus, I was alone, hurt, angry, disenchanted with churches and with God's people. I was a 1970's example of the Dones.

To create distance, I retreated to my Methodist roots. I was hired as the choir director at a local church. My musical talent allowed me to see God working in other people's lives but not get close enough to get burned. Much to my shame I worked as a Summer Youth Director at several churches throughout college. I made money to pay for school but I'm certain I did serious damage to the innocent faith of impressionable kids. God help them.

I drifted further and further away from Jesus, all the while talking to Him on occasion to mostly tell Him to leave me alone. I insulated myself from anyone that I suspected was a true Christian. In all my willful sin, rebellion, stubborn pride, and attempts to find happiness and true love outside of God, I was miserable. I had lost any sense of purpose. Still present on the surface, I made sure I had no real family of faith to challenge or encourage me. Church had failed me. Church was dead to me even when I was present. I was angry but I still checked the boxes on the outside.

Like me, I know many people that still go to church but, in their hearts, they are disconnected from God. They may go through the motions but there is little to no sense of relationship and no impetus to actively assist in the mission. That leads to the question, what is the Church to accomplish? How is it supposed to work?

John 20:21-22 – *"So Jesus said to them again, "Peace be with you; <u>as the Father has sent Me, I also send you.</u>" And when He had said this, He breathed on them and said to them, "Receive the Holy Spirit."*

After His resurrection Jesus gave this instruction and sending commission to His disciples. He sealed the commission with the impartation of the Holy Spirit. **Eph. 1:13**, *"In Him, you also, after listening to the message of truth, the gospel of your salvation--having also believed, you were sealed in Him with the Holy Spirit of promise."*

Jesus said, *"As the Father has sent Me, I also send you."* For what purpose? What is the function, the purpose, of the Church?

I have often been asked, "Can a nuclear family of believers in their home be an expression of the Church of Jesus Christ?" Yes! In fact, a Christian family *should* serve as an example of the Church. That is certainly a form that fulfills the essence. But a family that stays home on Sundays and does some religious things is not necessarily fulfilling the functions that Jesus requires of His Church. **James 2:17** tells us, *"Faith by itself, if it does not have works, is dead."*

We are not really being the Church if we merely check the boxes regarding the essence of Church. It's great to hang out together, especially when we are focused on Jesus. But the Church must also obey Jesus' instructions and commands according to the Bible. This leads to some other questions. Why does He call us to gather? What is the function of the Church? What is its purpose? This too is established in Scripture, and, like the essence, it never changes. **Ps. 33:11**, *"The counsel of the LORD stands forever, the plans of His heart from generation to generation."*

God does everything for His purpose. In **Eph. 3:10-11** God revealed the mystery of His purpose for the Church to Paul, *"so that the manifold wisdom of God might now be made known through the church to the rulers and the authorities in the heavenly places. This was in accordance with the eternal purpose which He carried out in Christ Jesus our Lord."*

To be Church means not just fulfilling the essence of the centrality of Christ through a gathering of people who share the same faith. The people gathered are also instructed to fulfill the function, the purpose set forth in Scripture. Remember, Church is not a human idea or institution that we get to define according to our own understanding. Nor is the Church headed by human beings. To be the Church in truth we must submit to the authority of Jesus Christ by reading, considering, and obeying the entirety of His revealed, infallible Word, the instructions of the Bible. The Church is called by Jesus to fulfill His purpose, not the purposes of humans – redeemed or not.

What then is the function of the church? We might say something like:

- to bring glory to Jesus,
- to be His body,
- to extend the Kingdom of God on the earth.

Those things are all true even if cloaked in archaic language that most people, including believers, do not really understand. What do they actually mean to us? What can we make of such broad theological statements? How do we bring Jesus glory in truth? What does it mean to be

His body? How are we to extend His Kingdom on earth? Reverting to my analogy, if the purpose of fishing is to catch fish, which are tangible and valuable resources, then what is the purpose of the Church?

As you might imagine, there are many instructions for the Church provided in Scripture. The entire New Testament is about the creation of the Church, the story of the early Church, the Lord's instructions for the churches, and descriptions and prophecies for the summation of the Church age when Jesus returns in glory for His Church.

There is a wonderful book that is available from Open Doors. The book is titled, *"Standing Strong Through The Storm,"* complied by Paul Estabrooks and Jim Cunningham. It is a training manual developed to equip believers to undergo persecution. In their examination of the Church in Scripture the authors present five basic functions that I'd like to quote and expand upon:

1. Evangelize (go and witness to the Good News, spread the truth) **Mark 16:15-16**, *"And He said to them, "Go into all the world and preach the gospel to all creation. He who has believed and has been baptized shall be saved; but he who has disbelieved shall be condemned."* **Acts 1:8**, *"but you will receive power when the Holy Spirit has come upon you; and you shall be My witnesses both in Jerusalem, and in all Judea and Samaria, and even to the remotest part of the earth."*

2. Make disciples (baptize, teach, train, live as examples) **Matt. 28:19-20**, *"Go therefore and make disciples of all the nations, baptizing them in the name of the Father and the Son and the Holy Spirit, teaching them to observe all that I commanded you; and lo, I am with you always, even to the end of the age."*

3. Minister to others (both in the family of God and in the world) **Gal. 6:10**, *"So then, while we have opportunity, let us do good to all people, and especially to those who are of the household of the faith."*

It's all the "one another's" of the Bible that are listed in Chapter 8. Then, employ these same practices with those that are outside of the household of faith. **Matt. 22:39**, *"You shall love your neighbor as yourself."*

4. <u>Fellowship together</u> – Read **Acts 2:42-47. Hebrews 10:23-25**, *"Let us hold fast the confession of our hope without wavering, for He who promised is faithful; and let us consider how to stimulate one another to love and good deeds, not forsaking our own assembling together, as is the habit of some, but encouraging one another; and all the more as you see the day drawing near."*

5. <u>Worship together</u> – **Matt. 4:10**, *"Then Jesus said to him, "Go, Satan! For it is written, 'YOU SHALL WORSHIP THE LORD YOUR GOD, AND SERVE HIM ONLY.'"* **John 4:23**, *"But an hour is coming, and now is, when the true worshipers will worship the Father in spirit and truth; for such people the Father seeks to be His worshipers."* **Colossians 3:12-17**, *"Put on then, as God's chosen ones, holy and beloved, compassionate hearts, kindness, humility, meekness, and patience, bearing with one another and, if one has a complaint against another, forgiving each other; as the Lord has forgiven you, so you also must forgive. And above all these put on love, which binds everything together in perfect harmony. And let the peace of Christ rule in your hearts, to which indeed you were called in one body. And be thankful. Let the word of Christ dwell in you richly, teaching and admonishing one another in all wisdom, singing psalms and hymns and spiritual songs, with thankfulness in your hearts to God. And whatever you do, in word or deed, do everything in the name of the Lord Jesus, giving thanks to God the Father through him."* This is true worship.

I'd like to add another function to their list as a summary:

6. <u>Demonstrate God's wisdom and authority</u> – **Eph. 3:8-11**, *"To me, though I am the very least of all the saints, this grace was given, to preach to the Gentiles the unsearchable riches of Christ, and to bring to light for everyone what is the plan of the mystery hidden for ages in God, who created all things, so that through the church the manifold wisdom of God might now be made known to the rulers and authorities in the heavenly places. This was according to the eternal purpose that he has realized in Christ Jesus our Lord."*

Maybe as you read and prayerfully consider this book you will identify a seventh so we will have a divine number! If so, let me know. I'd like to hear your thoughts.

For now, let's consider these six instructions to define the basic functions the Church is to pursue. When the Holy Spirit draws a group of people together for church (e.g., when true Church happens), all of these functions will be evident. These categories or groupings should encompass all the many and varied instructions and commands that are contained in the Bible regarding the purpose of Church.

For your consideration: which of these six functions do you think are more important? If you had to rank them, what order would you use? Stop here and give it a try. I'll wait.

Were you able to do it? I couldn't. From a study of scripture, I find no way to rank them according to which is more valuable or important to Jesus. It appears they are of equal importance. God is like that. He loves you and me, and the most wise and mature saint, and the worst sinner that was just saved while you were reading this with all His unconditional, boundless love at the same time. God is weird. He's different than us.

I believe our human tendency to judge God the same way we judge humans is one of the causes of problems in churches. We make value judgments based on our feelings, our beliefs, our own callings and mission, and other criteria that are most important to us. Again, God's thoughts are not our thoughts. Without a good systematic, biblical theology and understanding of the entire purpose of Church (or churches) in the Bible we can get unbalanced and make judgments that God would never make. There can be disconnects between believers and leaders and those that are being led. When that happens, the church is in danger of becoming unhealthy and divisive. When churches are unhealthy people get hurt and God's glory is diminished.

So how are we supposed to live our lives, be involved in a church, and make decisions about our thoughts and actions? The answer I hear most often from evangelical believers is (wait for it) … I live my life by biblical principles. Sounds good, doesn't it? Living by biblical principles implies that we each have the responsibility to read the Bible and make correct value judgments according to our own understanding. We're kings and priests unto God, right? C'mon. That's in the Bible.

While making decisions based on biblical principles sounds good and appeals to our own sense of worth, really that lifestyle is not biblical at all. At the peril of repeating myself please allow me to take one more pass at this subject. I do so because it is important.

> ***Proverbs 3:5-6***, *"Trust in the Lord with all your heart,*
> *and do not lean on your own understanding. In all your ways*
> *acknowledge him, and he will make straight your paths."*

Nowhere does the Bible teach us to live according to "biblical principles" as we understand them. We don't need to relive the error of the Pharisees. Instead of following the Living Word of God and trusting Him to direct our path, living by "biblical principles" places us in charge of our own lives. Worse, when we trust someone else to do this for us it puts someone(s) in charge of the church that is not Jesus.

Recently churches in the state where I live have been inviting an outspoken elected official to lecture from their pulpits on lightning rod social issues. This politician does have a strong, clear testimony of faith in Jesus Christ. Great! Check the box. His conservative views certainly appeal to some segments of Christians in our state, and he can really whip up a crowd. My question though is why is he being invited as a public speaker during Sunday morning worship? For what purpose? To catch fish? To glorify Jesus? To extend the Kingdom of God? Or something else? I can't help but wonder if these churches are virtue signaling to draw crowds and attention. I know. I'm judging my brother. Forgive me.

My concern is that every time this elected official speaks in a church the media are present. Immediately carefully edited video clips appear in the news that are designed to generate interest and ratings because his rhetoric stirs controversy, inflames tensions on all sides, and further divides people due to divergent viewpoints on social issues. How does this represent Jesus? How is it helping people come to know Him? How is this a function of Church?

If the Church is truly under the headship of Jesus Christ, we have to surrender our own thoughts and ideas to God's Word. If you ask people, "What is Church?" you'll hear all sorts of thoughts about its essence and function. But from Jesus' view according to the Bible, I submit the purpose of the Church may be summed up in the five functions of the Open Doors book and the additional number six I have proposed:

1. Evangelize
2. Make disciples
3. Minister
4. Fellowship
5. Worship
6. Demonstrate the wisdom & authority of God

As I wrote earlier, I do not claim to have the entirety of God's mind on His purpose for the Church. As I've demonstrated, that would be foolish and prideful. Nor do I claim that this list of functions is entirely accurate or complete. But it's a start and this list has the advantage of being drawn directly from the Bible.

In the next chapter we'll continue to examine the function of the Church and perhaps expand our understanding of how these functions are worked out practically.

Reflections

Ephesians Chapter 2 only has 22 verses. However, it is perhaps the most powerful description of the divine purposes of God regarding Jesus and His Church.

Please read and prayerfully consider this passage before going on to the next chapter. It may help to use the space below to outline and make notes.

_____

_____

_____

_____

_____

_____

_____

_____

_____

_____

_____

_____

_____

Chapter 11
Purpose

I n 2015 a tragic event occurred that would again challenge my understanding of the Church. A video surfaced that was recorded on a beach in Sirte, Libya. Twenty-one men in orange prison uniform were marched out onto the beach by armed ISIS (ISIL) militants dressed in black. All but one unfortunate Chadian were Coptic Christians from Egypt. These men were mostly poor and traveled to Libya for work in construction. It didn't work out well. Instead, one by one they refused to recant their faith and prayed to Jesus Christ as they were summarily beheaded in gruesome fashion. On camera, one of the terrorists asked the young man named Matthew from Chad, "Do you reject Christ?" "Their God is my God," he responded. He became one of the twenty-one men laying down their lives for their faith in Christ on that blood-stained beach.

The brutality of their captors and their bravery and dedication to Jesus and their Church in the face of certain death shocked the Church at large and the world. Their courage inspired many, including me to consider how I would respond if I were in their position. How did the ISIS militants identify them as Christians? Coptic Christians have a small cross tattooed on their right wrist. It brands them as followers of Jesus and members of the Coptic Church.

I'm not a big fan of tattoos and I don't have any. Let's face it, I'm old. I understand that places me outside of the majority culture in the USA today. However, I so wanted to identify with these brothers that I seriously considered having that little cross inked on my wrist. I don't have one yet for reasons that have to do with my current work for Jesus, but you never know. Stranger things have happened.

Why would anyone be so committed to Jesus Christ and to their Church family that they would visibly brand themselves as believers in a hostile environment and refuse to renounce Jesus Christ on penalty of death? It's worth considering as we examine the function of the Church. What would you give or endure for Jesus and your brothers and sisters in Christ?

In the last chapter we examined a list of the essential, unchanging purposes that define the function of the Church.

1. Evangelize
2. Make disciples
3. Minister
4. Fellowship
5. Worship
6. Demonstrate the wisdom & the authority of God

The Bible indicates that each of these functions is equally important. When Jesus is in control of the church, all these functions will be evident. It is not a stretch to say that this should be the normal church experience. Take a minute and compare that to your church experience. Who is in control?

> *"And he put all things under his feet and gave him as head over all things to the church, which is his body, the fullness of him who fills all in all."*
> ### *Eph. 1:22-23*

When Jesus is not the One in charge in a church, other purposes will command center stage and place additional demands on the members.

At the end of the last chapter, I recommended reading and meditating on Ephesians Chapter Two. As a practical example, let's review this passage and see if we can identify the functions of the Church at work in Paul's and the Lord's treatise delivered to the Church in Ephesus.

Salvation - Death To Life

¹And you were dead in your trespasses and sins, ²in which you formerly walked according to the course of this world, according to the prince of the power of the air, of the spirit that is now working in the sons of disobedience. ³Among them we too all formerly lived in the lusts of our flesh, indulging the desires of the flesh and of the mind, and were by nature children of wrath, even as the rest. ⁴But God, being rich in mercy, because of His great love with which He loved us, ⁵even when we were dead in our transgressions, made us alive together with Christ (by grace you have been saved),

1. Evangelize

A. Before we believed in Jesus, we were like the walking dead because of our sins. That's why Jesus commands us in **Mark 16:15** to, *"Go into all the world and preach the Gospel to all creation."*

B. We were in bondage not just to sin and the sentence of death but to Satan and his world forces of darkness. True believers will want to share God's goodness, love, light, and salvation with others.

C. We believe that without Jesus as Lord, people will suffer eternal separation from God and unending torment.

D. The Great Commandment is to love God and love others. We must love others enough to tell them the Good News. In doing so, we extend the grace of God as it was freely given to us for our salvation.

How the Church evangelizes can take many forms including community outreach, personal witness, demonstrations of God's love and grace, etc. Early believers shared Scripture from memory to evangelize since they didn't have the Bible on their phones. It's actually easier to evangelize than we generally think and fear.

2. Worship

⁶and raised us up with Him, and seated us with Him in the heavenly places in Christ Jesus, ⁷so that in the ages to come He might show the surpassing riches of His grace in kindness toward us in Christ Jesus. ⁸For by grace you have been saved through faith; and that not of yourselves, it is the gift of God; ⁹not as a result of works, so that no one may boast.

We worship God because He is entirely good. A.W. Pink in his book *Exposition of the Gospel of John* defined worship this way, *"A redeemed heart occupied with God, expressing itself in adoration and thanksgiving...Worship, then, is the occupation of the heart with a known God. Everything which attracts the flesh and its senses, detracts from real worship."* This is a helpful understanding as we consider how we worship God in church.

3. Ministry

¹⁰For we are His workmanship, created in Christ Jesus for good works, which God prepared beforehand so that we would walk in them.

We find two Greek words in the New Testament that are translated as "ministry": *diakonia* (service) and *leitourgia* (priestly service, esp. to other believers). We see the early church in the Book of Acts serving food to one other, sharing all things with those in need, raising funds for the support of persecuted saints in Jerusalem, and caring for the sick and dying.

We should note that it wasn't just their fellow believers that received ministry. The early church practiced what they had witnessed Jesus doing and what they read in scripture. Jesus gave His disciples the Parable of the Good Samaritan on purpose. Faithful churches do good works for one another, for their communities, and even for their enemies. They do what Jesus did and walk out what He taught. That's what the early churches in Book of Acts Church were known for. The Church had a good reputation in the community just as Jesus did even though enemies remained. As a result, more people were drawn to Jesus as Lord because they experienced the love of God in action. **Acts 5:13** tells us, *"The people held them (the Church) in high esteem."*

It can be argued that being held in high esteem is not a universal benchmark that can or should be applied to the Church in every time, season, and location. After all, Jesus Himself said in **Luke 21:17**, *"You will be hated by all for my name's sake."* But hated by people, society, and even by nations or not, the Bible is clear that the Church should always do good to one another and to our neighbors. We are to give no just cause for accusation or guilt in our intent and actions. How are churches doing in that regard?

One can easily and fairly note that the reputation of the church is quite different today throughout much of the world than it was shortly after its inception. We need to ask ourselves, do our churches fulfill the purpose of ministry as Jesus intends? If not, perhaps the next function could be employed to fix that.

4. Make Disciples

[11] Therefore remember that formerly you, the Gentiles in the flesh, who are called "Uncircumcision" by the so-called "Circumcision," which is performed in the flesh by human hands–[12] remember that you were at that time separate from Christ, excluded from the commonwealth of Israel, and strangers to the covenants of promise, having no hope and without God in the world. [13] But now in Christ Jesus you who formerly were far off have been brought near by the blood of Christ.

Discipleship is one of those words that is not used outside of the Church. Discipleship simply means teaching and training people to live faithfully as Jesus followers. The Church has been delegated responsibility by Jesus for people that become Christians. That responsibility involves each faithful believer being engaged in one-on-one, small setting, and large group modeling, teaching, and training in all the attributes of God and the commandments of Jesus. The Bible specifically addresses baptism, Christian living, the desire for and exercise of spiritual gifts, preaching and teaching, church discipline, instruction in righteousness, and more. Churches should be faithful to encourage and promote these practices among the saints.

5. Fellowship

[14]For He Himself is our peace, who made both groups into one and broke down the barrier of the dividing wall, [15]by abolishing in His flesh the enmity, which is the Law of commandments contained in ordinances, so that in Himself He might make the two into one new man, thus establishing peace, [16]and might reconcile them both in one body to God through the cross, by it having put to death the enmity. [17]AND HE CAME AND PREACHED PEACE TO YOU WHO WERE FAR AWAY, AND PEACE TO THOSE WHO WERE NEAR; [18]for through Him we both have our access in one Spirit to the Father. [19]So then you are no longer strangers and aliens, but you are fellow citizens with the saints, and are of God's household,

Fellowship is the sharing of everything in common, taking the Lord's Supper (communion) together, spending time with each other outside of organized meetings, having meals together, sharing the celebration and grief of life events, intercessory prayer, and more – all in the peace of Christ. For your own fun and curiosity, do a word search and see how many times the word "fellowship" is mentioned in the New Testament and pay attention to the context.

6. Demonstrate the authority of God

20having been built on the foundation of the apostles and prophets, Christ Jesus Himself being the corner stone,

The Church exists to demonstrate obedience to God's authority. Christians are instructed to be obedient both to King Jesus and to human spiritual authority He appoints in the Church as indicated in the Bible. Jesus is the Good Shepherd, and He appoints under-shepherds to assist with the functions. We are to respond in willing submission in faith that Jesus is the Head of the Church. Anything else that is a requirement of man, including the misuse of delegated power is coercion.

7. Worship again

21in whom the whole building, being fitted together, is growing into a holy temple in the Lord, 22in whom you also are being built together into a dwelling of God in the Spirit.

How amazing is it that when we gather God shows up and makes His presence known? He promises that He is always there, moving among those who make up His Church. I wonder, can you sense Him in your meetings? Do you experience His leading and direction? Can you at least occasionally feel Him? I know. I just set off alarm bells and triggers. I get it. Our feelings are subjective. But it would be strange when your earthly father is in the room not to at least experience His presence in some way or see some evidence that He is there. How much more when the Creator of the Universe is with us?

There's one important sign of a functioning church that I have not included in the list of Church functions. Prayer. You may wonder why?

Some years ago, before I was asked to pastor our church, I was appointed an Elder. I served with the Pastor and other elders as we tried to faithfully guide and lead the church in the way we believe God would have us go. As you might imagine, not everyone always agreed with some of the decisions we made or the direction we pursued.

There is a faithful man of God that has been part of our fellowship since the very early days. He is someone with influence in the church. That's the way God designed the Church. Not everyone is called to hold an office or title, but we are all called to walk in integrity before God. People that are faithful in their calling are often people of influence. They don't need a title or other recognition. When they speak you are wise to listen because you know they've been with Jesus. This man is one of those people.

He asked to meet with the Elders regarding a decision we had made that I have long since forgotten. But I have not forgotten the challenge he issued to us that day. He asked us a simple question about whatever it was. He merely asked, "Have you prayed about this?"

Sounds silly, right? We're the Elders after all. We're charged with praying about all matters related to the church. The reaction was immediate and not kind. It was defensive. Was he charging us with a sin? Was he suggesting we were leading the people astray? Was he suggesting we were in doctrinal error? We were offended. We deflected. We explained our thinking. But there was one thing we didn't do. We didn't answer his question. We couldn't answer him honestly because the truth was, no. We had not prayed about it. We mistakenly assumed the wisdom of God was vested in us.

I have never felt so convicted. It was a simple question presented without judgment or attitude. The Holy Spirit empowered that simple question, and then He did what only He can do. He convicted me and the other elders of our sin, our failure to pray and seek God's direction in everything. I'm sure we made that decision based on "biblical principles." Pride really does go before the fall. I've learned over the course of my life that humility requires humiliation. It's not fun, but the scripture tells us that humility is necessary to please God.

God used this faithful saint's simple question to change everything about the way that our church leadership functioned. Prayer is a powerful thing, and he was a praying man. I dedicated myself that day to becoming like him in that regard. We are dear friends and brothers in Christ to this day.

I didn't list prayer separately as a function of the Church because it is so deeply embedded in executing all the other functions. Perhaps that is an oversight on my part. Please don't miss the importance of prayer like I did for so many years. When you are in a place of concern or questioning, when you have a decision to make, please ask yourself and perhaps others this question. Have you prayed about it? Then don't move until you have an answer. When you pray God will certainly answer.

What is Church? We know Church is genuine when the presence of God and the life of Jesus are seen among us and experienced by others, both inside and outside the church. God is Spirit. He is supernatural. We cannot control Him. In the Church of Jesus Christ, there will be evidence that God is with us and that He is in control.

Reflections

We've covered essence and function. Before we get into form or forms, we're going to take another pause and examine the importance of God's Love Experienced In Community. We'll see how God's purpose for the Church is revealed and demonstrated in the world today through His great love. Before you go on take a few minutes to pray and think through these questions.

How have you seen God's love displayed in the Church?

_____

_____

_____

_____

How have you seen God's love denied in the Church?

_____

_____

_____

_____

How important is God's love to the Church?

_____

_____

_____

_____

Chapter 12
Seeking A Simple Answer

By now you've read though a lot of teaching and scripture analysis. We started all of this with what appears to be a simple question. What is Church? In trying to answer that question adequately the format I have presented may seem too structured, complicated, and perhaps a little rigid. I lean more organic in real life. Can we boil all of this down to a simple way of looking at Church? Yes. God conveniently has already done it for us in I Corinthians 13. The answers we are seeking really are found in one word – Love.

Before we dive too deeply into the love pool, I'd like to first clear a path through the jumble of our current situation so we can more clearly see where we are going. Please indulge me and I promise to get to the point as quickly as I'm able and back to the pool.

Unless you've been living on an island with no external communication you've likely encountered the word deconstruction used in terms of faith and Christianity. You may even be in your own process of deconstruction as you read this. In certain circles of the church someone engaged in deconstructing their faith, religion, denomination, or the cultural focus of their church experience may be considered dangerous, foolish, or downright heretical. What exactly is deconstruction regarding the Christian faith?

Mark Hackett, a millennial Christian writer defines it this way, *"Faith deconstruction is the systematic pulling apart of one's belief system for examination. For Christians, that can mean a wide array of questions ranging from the theological to the practical. Faith deconstruction is confronting hard questions and grievous experiences that a believer has suppressed for years, forcing them to finally deal with the doubts and concerns that have always been there, lurking in the shadows. Removing false teachings or misapplications of the Gospel is the primary goal."*

It's obvious by now that I am not a millennial. But I am no stranger to the struggles that my dear younger brothers and sisters in the Lord are going through. You've been reading some of my story in this book. I hope and pray you can relate to some of these experiences and learn from them.

I wouldn't have known the term deconstruction at the time but a generation that had grown up with a wide variety of church experiences ran headlong into Jesus and certainly began what would now be considered deconstructing our faith. Once saved we desired to know all about Jesus. We desired to do things the way He did them; to know and practice everything He said, to treat people the way He treated them, and to help other people find the Jesus we knew and loved.

In my circle of the newly committed we read the Bible daily, fervently, from cover to cover, discussed the scriptures and our experiences with our friends. We gathered with like-minded believers from every background, denomination, and ethnicity for prayer, worship, and community as often as possible. We found Jesus together and we experienced the power and presence of God the Father, Son, and Holy Spirit in a way that we had read and been taught in the Bible but had never really known in practice. It was a wonderful, heady, scary, and exciting time. Still, not everything was roses.

What we didn't find in our searching, our deconstruction of the religions and denominations we had grown up with, were many mature Christians that were willing to engage with us and help us sort through these things. In other words, we didn't find much love for our kind. Our parents were mostly pleased with the change in our attitudes if not our appearance. But they didn't know how to answer our questions or guide us beyond their own church experiences and expectations.

In our enthusiasm we turned to the churches we had grown up in expecting to find mature leaders that would meet us with acceptance and spiritual guidance. That proved to be very unsatisfying. For the most part we encountered stubborn people; church leaders, and church members that were deeply embedded in their own social church cultures that excluded more than included us and other new believers that were coming to Christ by the thousands. We were stung by rejection, disappointment, and frustration.

Some churches were more welcoming than others, thank God. But the lack of grace, acceptance, compassion, love, enthusiasm, and patience required for making disciples were in short supply. Why? Because the church at large in the Western world, the USA, and the American South already had its own religious cultures that did not allow for inquiry, examination, challenge, change, or movement.

Serendipitously, as God moved in the world at large some more mature adults were also coming to Jesus even if in smaller numbers. These new, refreshed, or revived believers also pursued what might be characterized now as deconstruction for many of the same reasons as the Jesus People generation. Their enthusiasm for Jesus and His Word led them likewise directly to the scriptures, the study of Jesus' life, and the deep pursuit of intimacy with Him. For perhaps the first time we all pursued the Bible and the Holy Spirit to be our guides even as my generation learned from other, more mature believers.

Churches and denominations entrenched in their own traditions did not like it and did not respond well. Those challenged by the Jesus Movement turned away from the opportunity for reformation. As church doors closed, young and more mature Christians together sought community with others that had also been quickened to life in Jesus. New groups gathered and over time new churches formed.

Now here we are again at another inflection point that I believe is caused and led by Jesus through the Holy Spirit. The circumstances in our nation and our churches today are quite different than those in the 1960's and 1970's, but the yearning for genuine faith, practice, acceptance, and loving community in the Church is once again burning hot. There is a new generation of young people that were likewise raised in church cultures that are threatened by both a rapid decline of Christian influence in society and legitimate problems and concerns that need to be addressed within the church itself. How will the currently established church respond this time? Are we willing to examine our systems, practices, and man-centered church cultures and surrender to the sovereignty of God and His Kingdom on Earth as Jesus intended? Remember His declaration in the Gospels, *"Repent, for the kingdom of heaven is at hand."* It still is. Will we repent from our sins and return to dependence on His Lordship above all else?

Time will tell. One thing is sure. Jesus will not abandon His Church. He will build His Kingdom and His Church. All the powers of Hell and Earth will never thwart His will. Our charge is to be ready when He returns. More on that later. For now, let's think more about God's love as it relates to the Church.

Reflections

Jesus prophesies the future in **Matt. 24:10-12**, *"And then many will fall away and betray one another and hate one another. And many false prophets will arise and lead many astray. And because lawlessness will be increased, the love of many will grow cold."*

Pray and ask the Lord, Are we there yet? Is the love of many growing ever colder?

How is the knowledge that the love of many will grow cold affecting me?

_____

_____

_____

_____

_____

How is affecting the church?

_____

_____

_____

_____

_____

_____

Chapter 13
The Answer Is Love

I believe the study of essence, function, form, and other aspects of Jesus' Church as we shall see in later chapters may be helpful during this season of opportunity for the Church. If we are not careful, even with good intentions we run the risk of becoming modern day Pharisees, building our own kingdom instead of His. Creating a God and a church in our own image, focusing on the works of our own understanding and effort rather than on Jesus and the power of the timeless and living Word of God. Is it possible in the process of deconstruction, examination, and search for Christ's Church to only find later to our shame that we merely ended up with another set of man-centered rules, traditions, and cultures that also missed the mark? I'm concerned that has happened to my generation.

Sadly, both the Bible and Church history are littered with the same disturbing pattern. God moves in love, grace, and mercy to save. People repent and respond. Things are great for a while. Manmade constructs emerge often with good intentions to sustain holiness and faithfulness. Over time dependence on God wanes. People are turned off and turn away from God. God intervenes again. Wash, rinse, repeat.

One of my goals is to help you, the current generation, avoid repeating the mistakes of the past. The Church Jesus is building is preparing for His return. We don't know when, but we are certain His return is nearer now that when the Church was formed. One day soon the age of grace will come to an end. The stakes are high. Lives and eternal destinies are at risk for those that do not know Jesus. What is Church and how can we participate with Him as Jesus makes His Bride ready for His return?

I wrote this book in the hope that better understanding will help bring clarity. As I indicated earlier, a biblical study in Western, didactic teaching fashion like this may seem as if the concept and practice of Church is too complicated to understand and practice, and the process of discovery is too rigid to be true to the Spirit of the Living God.

As God the Creator is all-powerful and sovereign in all things, is there perhaps a simple summary of the essence, function, and nature of Jesus' Church that we can cling to? With humility and great fear of God I would like to propose an answer to the question, "What is Church?" **Church is the love of God expressed in community.** When the Great Commandment & the Great Commission of Jesus are lived out together by believers in community, in reality that is Church. **I John 3:18**, *"Little children, let us not love with word or with tongue, but in deed and truth."*

> *"The first Christians didn't out-argue pagans – they outlived*
> *them. Christianity made no attempts to conquer paganism and*
> *dead religion blow by blow. Instead, the Christians of the first*
> *century outthought, out prayed, and outlived the unbelievers.*
> *Their weapons were positive, not negative. As far as we know they*
> *did not hold protests or conduct boycotts. They did not put on*
> *campaigns to try and unseat the emperor. Instead, they prayed and*
> *preached and proclaimed the message of Christ, put to death on*

The Answer Is Love | 107

*the cross, risen from the dead, and ready to change lives. And they
backed up their message with actions: giving, loving."
The Upside Down Church, Greg Laurie*

Stop and think for a minute. When was the last time you told someone with conviction that God loves them? That Jesus is God. That He came to earth and lived a perfect life. That He bore all our sins and was put to death on the cross. That He rose from the dead. That He now lives in Heaven and is able to save anyone and everyone that believes in Him and trusts Him with their life? How long has it been since you told someone that?

That's the Gospel, the Good News. Jesus promises that when we deliver this message for Him, He will always be there to work with us and confirm it with signs and wonders. The words are important. God's power always accompanies what He says. The spiritual and physical power necessary to effect change occurs when God speaks because what He says comes from Who He is. The power of the words is in His nature, His character, His very being. That's true when we use His words too.

The church of Jesus Christ is the visible demonstration that the Gospel is true, and that Jesus is the One True God who loves. Our ability to make an impact on the world and those around us is dependent on our being positively different. When we are the Church as Jesus lays it out in the Bible, we don't have to try to be different or advertise it to people. We already are different. We just need to be obedient to Jesus and not compromise our witness because of resistance from the world and the culture around us. We need to stop being ashamed of Jesus. We need to stop being ashamed of being His Body, the Ekklesia, the called-out ones, His church. Especially when some of the actions of "the church" make us ashamed.

Jesus said that His disciples are to be salt and light. If our standard of morality is compromised, then we are no longer salt. If our lives do not shine with the life of Christ, then we are not light. Whatever compromise we allow that deviates from God's standard, whatever darkness we personally entertain, also enters into the community of Christ followers. It weakens the Church. It cheapens our witness to those we are charged to reach with Jesus' Gospel of love, repentance, forgiveness, redemption, and joy!

The Church is empowered to speak to those who are without Christ and say, *"Look here, the light of Jesus is brighter than your darkness. The love of Christ is better than the wickedness that is all around you. The hope of salvation that Jesus secured for you on the cross gives the meaning you are seeking in your life. The love of God compels us to tell you of His great love and sacrifice on your behalf. Turn to Jesus and be saved from the death and destruction that is all around you. Turn to Jesus and find peace and refuge in times of fear, sadness, and insecurity. There is no other way to be saved from this. Turn to Jesus. He alone is God. He alone is Lord. He alone is your Savior. He is your King. He is your Master, your Fortress, your Shield, your Defender. He is the lover of your soul. Jesus is God. He loves you with everlasting, unconditional, and undying love. He's waiting for you with arms wide open. Turn to Jesus and be saved! We are His witnesses. Look at the blessing of God among us and join us."*

That's why the Church is here. The Church is Jesus' plan to take His message of love and salvation by grace to all people everywhere in this hurting and dying world. There is no Plan B. There is no other option. We can't reinvent the Church to meet our own desires, to assuage our own guilt, or to insulate us from being hurt again. We can't make the Church our own playground or redesign it in our image. The Church is the Body of Christ on earth. The Church Body takes its orders from the Head, who is Jesus Christ alone. He has been given all power and authority over everything that walks, talks, moves, lives, and breathes. He commands the Church because it is His Body. He fills the Church with His presence, His power, and His love. It is our great privilege to know

Jesus, to read, hear, and understand His words. To reflect on what He says. To obey Him, and to experience His manifest presence.

When we do, what amazing joy is ours! What amazing love falls on us. What amazing power is displayed through us, His tribe, His people, His family. What amazing grace comes to all who are touched by His great love. First to the Church, and then to the unbeliever who sees the reality of Jesus in the love that is shown in our communities. To the one that is moved mentally, spiritually, and emotionally by God's great mercy and compassion. To the one that feels for the first time their human spirit begins to come alive as the Holy Spirit moves in and takes control. The miracle of salvation occurs, and the Holy Spirit breathes life into a mortal body. Then, with all heaven rejoicing, these newly born-again individuals join the chorus of the angels and the Church universal singing the praises of God and worshiping together in His presence.

What is Church? It isn't a building. It isn't just an individual person that follows Jesus. It isn't only what happens on Sunday morning in certain parts of the world. Instead, Church is two, or three, or a hundred, or a thousand, or tens of thousands of voices raised in unison all singing together, *"How Great is Our God. Sing with me; How Great is Our God. And all will see, How Great, How Great is our God!"* © Chris Tomlin, Jesse Reeves, Ed Cash, sixsteps/Sparrow 2014

When our hearts are joined together in that chorus the power and the glory of God comes down and the earth is filled with His presence. His Kingdom comes and His will is done here on earth just as it is in Heaven. That's Church. That should be the longing of every Jesus follower whenever we gather to worship Him. Listen to this description of the Church from **Hebrews 12:18-24**.

> *"For you have not come to what may be touched, a blazing fire and*
> *darkness and gloom and a tempest and the sound of a trumpet and a*
> *voice whose words made the hearers beg that no further messages be*

*spoken to them. For they could not endure the order that was given,
"If even a beast touches the mountain, it shall be stoned." Indeed, so
terrifying was the sight that Moses said, "I tremble with fear." But
you have come to Mount Zion and to the city of the living God, the
heavenly Jerusalem, and to innumerable angels in festal gathering,
and to the assembly of the firstborn who are enrolled in heaven,
and to God, the judge of all, and to the spirits of the righteous made
perfect, and to Jesus, the mediator of a new covenant, and to the
sprinkled blood that speaks a better word than the blood of Abel."*

This is not Old Testament stuff. This is the New Testament description of the New Covenant Kingdom of God that Jesus brought from Heaven to Earth. He grants the Kingdom of God to everyone that accepts His call for salvation. He gives His Kingdom on earth to the care of His Church. In the very next chapter, the first verse in **Hebrews 13:1** is an instruction to the Church, *"Keep on loving each other as brothers and sisters."* That's His command because this is the evidence that the Church is real.

How important is it that the Church be defined by love expressed in community? Love in community is the very life of the Church and the evidence that Jesus is Lord. It is the hope of the world. But wait, I hear you. The Bible says that Jesus is the hope of the world. Yes! That's true. Jesus tells us in His Word that the Church is the Body of Christ, His Body, here and now for all the world to witness. The Hope of the World is expressed in the Church.

Can you see now why Satan would do everything he can to divide us? To separate us from our Christian family? To frighten us into inaction? To compromise our witness? To harm, discourage, depress, and demoralize us? To lull us to sleep? To stir up anger and strife without reconciliation? To conform us to the world of darkness that he has constructed for his own devilish purpose. To cause us to bow to his will instead of the will of God? The Church is the only human force that has the understanding, the will, and the supernatural ability to stand against his evil power and overcome him because we are inhabited and empowered by the Spirit of God.

"And they have conquered him by the blood of the Lamb and by the word of their testimony, for they loved not their lives even unto death."
Rev. 12:11

How important is Church in our world today? Despite what you may have heard, it has never been more important. It has never been more critical that we understand the Church, and that we practice the genuine faith and love that has been handed down to us over the centuries by faithful men and women who paid the price, who bled and died for Jesus and for these truths. It is time for the Church to come together as one and take its place in the war for the souls of men, women, boys, and girls from all tribes and nations and peoples and languages.

This requires great love; the amazing, unending love of God for His people. It is the same love that Jesus displayed on the cross as He gave up His life so that we might be saved. God's love is most fully experienced and expressed in the community of people that Jesus saves, calls, and empowers to follow Him. That is Church.

Reflections

How has your experience of God's love in community affected your life in a positive way?

_____

_____

_____

How has your experience of the lack of God's love in community affected your life in a negative way?

_____

_____

_____

What do you feel called by God to do to express His love to others?

_____

_____

_____

Is that best done individually or in community?

_____

_____

_____

Chapter 14
Form

In previous sections we referenced deconstruction. When you deconstruct a house (Demo Day!) that is not the end unless you plan to leave a mess or an empty lot. Likewise, the next step for responsible church and faith deconstructors is reconstruction. This is where the form of the Church comes into focus. There has to be a plan somewhere.

At the end of my college career, I was pretty far away from God, even though He remained near to me. God takes our confession or belief, repentance, and commitment a lot more seriously than we do. He is faithful when we are not. I wouldn't learn this for about 12 years.

Fast forward. I went on the graduate school and received a master's degree in music. I got hired, worked, and traveled in the entertainment business. In all of this I did all I could to continually push God away from my being and my consciousness. It didn't work but I was stubborn. Then I met Pam, the amazing woman that would become my wife.

God sent Pam into my life when I was at my lowest point. Like me she too had a church and salvation background. Like me she wasn't walking with Jesus. Unlike me, she still knew what was true and what wasn't. Still, that wasn't what drew me back to Him. It was the love we had for each other. We'd both been in other relationships, but this was different. From the beginning there was a powerful, binding, enduring love that we both knew was beyond our own capability.

We met and married nine months later. The road home to Jesus took a little longer. God was very intent on reclaiming us. He worked through the circumstances of our life until we could no longer deny Him. Standing on a pier in Maui, Hawaii I finally said, "Enough. I surrender. From today on I will give you everything I have." Shortly after that Pam made the same commitment. Like the prodigal of scripture, we were back in the family of God. Now we just had to figure out how to live.

Eventually God led us to Durham, NC. While staying temporarily with Pam's wonderful Christian parents we began to look for A) a church, B) a place to live, and C) work with income. Her very practical dad pointed out that most people do that in reverse order.

We came from different denominational backgrounds. We knew we wanted something different, and we began to pray for direction. We tried visiting one church. When we explained what we thought we were looking for they politely but firmly told us to go elsewhere. As we say in the South, "Well bless your hearts." This was 1985, the dark ages before the internet. We had to ask and trust God for direction. On TV there was a program called The 700 Club. Christian programming was new to us, and we were skeptical of religion. However, CBN had a network called Operation Blessing that provided relief and support "with the love of Jesus." That impressed us so we called them. We told them we were in Durham, NC and needed a church. They recommended Christian Assembly Church and Pastor Paul Gordon. We've been there ever since.

Interesting, Christian Assembly (CA) was known as a reformed charismatic church. You may remember the people I reacted against that pushed me away from God were from the same stream. Now God used "those people" to draw me back to His Church. This time, love and acceptance made the difference. Funny how we get all caught up in the form of church and forget that it's all about Jesus anyway. Let's take some time to look more closely into the idea of church form or forms.

We're pretty far down the road of determining what is Church. Love expressed in community is the way I've chosen to describe it. But what does that look like in reality? To determine that in your context it may be helpful to examine the form of church.

The essence and the function are established by God in the Bible with Jesus as the Head of the Church. That part should be settled according to scripture. On the other hand, the form or forms may be as varied as necessary to fulfill the essence and the function as Jesus alone sees fit for the moment. It is important once again to remember here that the Church is not man-led, but God led. Some people have a lot of creativity and imagination that are no doubt gifts from God. But how those thoughts and creative ideas are stewarded is important. The form of the church over time has been varied and constantly changing under the leadership of individuals and groups. Those in charge should operate under the inspiration of the Holy Spirit working through people. In the end though, any church form is valid only as Jesus determines and approves.

Many people have remarked over the centuries that it would have been so much easier if God had just clearly laid out an unchanging pattern and form for the Church in the New Testament. He certainly could have done that. In the Old Testament, God was very specific with His instructions for the location, construction, organization, and practices of the Tabernacle and then the Temple. In great detail God laid out the facility, the organizational structure, and the practices of the place where He chose for His Spirit to dwell with people. The form of both the Tabernacle and the Temple were very clearly defined and enforced. Even with that kind of specificity of instruction the relationship between God and mankind was not made perfect.

When Jesus came to establish the Kingdom of God on earth, the Church became the New Covenant expression of God's family. Instead of an intricately constructed place of worship, the Holy Spirit of God now dwells in born-again believers. And unlike the Temple, in His Church the Lord purposely did not specifically lay out a single form that we're to follow.

In one of the most remarkable recorded encounters between Jesus and any person in the Bible Jesus reveals Himself as Messiah to a Samaritan woman. Shocking. When she questions him about the Temple in Jerusalem and whether people like her are required to worship there, He speaks to her of the Church that He will soon establish.

"Jesus said to her, "Woman, believe me, the hour is coming when neither on this mountain nor in Jerusalem will you worship the Father. You worship what you do not know; we worship what we know, for salvation is from the Jews. But the hour is coming, and is now here, when the true worshipers will worship the Father in spirit and truth, for the Father is seeking such people to worship him. God is spirit, and those who worship him must worship in spirit and truth. The woman said to him, "I know that Messiah is coming (he who is called Christ). When he comes, he will tell us all things." Jesus said to her, "I who speak to you am he." **John 1:21-26**

This is perhaps the most profound and revealing thing Jesus ever told anyone about Himself and what we have come to know as the Church of Jesus Christ. Amazing. God is always at work in the world in Spirit and in Truth. The Church, the Body of Christ, is made up of living people under the headship of Jesus, the Living God. Just as salvation is not simply a single point in time experience but rather the establishment of an ongoing, dynamic relationship with God, the Church at large is likewise not a single point in time experience but rather an ongoing, dynamic relationship with Jesus, the Living Word of God. We are always to be guided by the Holy Spirit.

Ephesians 4:11-16 frames it this way, *"And he gave the apostles, the prophets, the evangelists, the shepherds and teachers, to equip the saints for the work of ministry, for building up the body of Christ, until we all attain* *to the unity of the faith and of the knowledge of the Son of God, to mature manhood, to the measure of the stature of the fullness of Christ, so that we may no longer be children, tossed to and fro by the waves and carried about by every wind of doctrine, by human cunning, by craftiness in deceitful schemes. Rather, speaking the truth in love, we are to grow up in every way into him who is the head, into Christ, from whom the whole body, joined and held together by every joint with which it is equipped, when each part is working properly, makes the body grow so that it builds itself up in love."*

Until Jesus returns, He is always at work in the world and in His Church. As times and seasons change and as the Church develops and eventually grows up, the form of the Church may change, even in our lifetime, to meet the need of the moment as Jesus sees fit. Meanwhile the essence and the function will never change until the Lord returns. We're not there yet, but Maranatha, which means, "Come soon Lord Jesus." In the meantime, we need to take care to be faithful to Jesus and to His Word.

The best way we can do that is in community with other faithful believers. Like it or not, that's the Church. It's the only option that is true to God's plan. With that in mind, let's look more in depth at form or perhaps more accurately, forms.

Reflections

What kinds of church forms have you personally experienced?

_____

_____

_____

_____

What did you like about them?

_____

_____

_____

_____

What did you dislike?

_____

_____

_____

_____

Do you have a preference?

_____

_____

_____

_____

_____

Chapter 15

Which Form?

A s we've noted, in the Bible God isn't terribly specific about how we do church. The church can meet in an owned facility, a leased or shared building, in a field, in a stadium, in a cave, under a tree, or in a home. COVID taught us that the church can even meet online. We can meet on Sunday or any other day of the week. The ways we worship can be incredibly varied if they conform to the essence and the function. There are many examples in the Bible. The question then is, how do I know where I fit in? Is any form valid and approved by Jesus? For our American readers, let's start where we live.

From the beginning of European migration to America when people thought of church, they usually meant a building in a town, a community, or a neighborhood where Christians gathered to worship Jesus. That's the way it worked in the experience of the first Christians that emigrated here. Most congregations in the early days of the nation would be considered very small by Christians today. A church with more than 100 attendees was considered a very large church. In the last few decades when most of our current population was born there has been a significant shift in our experience and expectations.

There is one form of what we now term Evangelical Christianity that dominates the American Christian mind and ideal of what church should be. It's the mega church. As one of our former congregants noted on his way out the door, *"It's just so exciting over there!"* And certainly, it is exciting to be part of a large church movement with hundreds and even thousands of other believers gathering in spectacular fashion.

Among church leaders it is little known or cared that 90% of churches in America are under 250 in attendance. 70% have 100 or fewer worship service attendees. Large churches with 500 or more average attendance comprise only 2-3%. Megachurches with 2,000 or more attendees are a whopping 0.5% of total churches in the USA. While smaller churches generally have higher commitment levels according to spiritual health studies, the dynamic that matters most socially is that larger churches are more likely to grow numerically. (Information courtesy of Hartford Institute for Religion Research, 2020) People want to go where something big is happening.

Churches in financially self-sufficient, unrestricted societies like ours are able to consider and support the large buildings, large budgets, paid staff, necessary technology, well-funded programs for every subgroup, expensive community outreaches, and large foreign mission programs that require vast amounts of resources in people and money to establish and maintain. To the stereotypical, modern American mindset the mega church model is exciting! However, Americans are not alone or even in the lead in this recent church form phenomenon.

Among the ten largest churches in the world in attendance the top eight are in South Korea, India, Chile, Indonesia, Nigeria, and the Philippines. Only the smallest two on the world top ten list are in the USA. Each of the American megachurches has average weekly attendance that only amounts to 10-11% of the size of the congregation when compared to the world's largest church that is in South Korea. No wonder many church leaders consider the South Korean church or some of the African and Latin American churches the model for evangelical churches!

As humans we're impressed by size and sheer numbers. It must mean these churches and their leaders are doing church right. Isn't that a sign of God's blessing? Perhaps. But we shouldn't assume our conclusion is entirely accurate if we trust the Bible. **Isaiah 55:8**, *"For my thoughts are not your thoughts, neither are your ways my ways, declares the Lord."* That's literally what God said so we need to believe Him. OK then, if that's not the divine model what other forms should we consider?

There is another important, certainly larger in scope, and often under-considered church form that is clearly meeting the essence and function of Church. We may not be familiar with it because this church form is defined in a very different way than most of us have experienced. We find it practiced most often in and around Asia and the Middle East. These churches are much smaller individually and much larger corporately. This form has been designated as Church Planting Networks. Here's how they work.

Rather than an independent or denominationally organized structure this church form has an organic regionality. The leadership structure is not defined or dominated by pastoral leadership but rather the form is applied from the Ephesians 4 pattern of leaders working together in harmony.

"And he gave the apostles, the prophets, the evangelists, the shepherds (pastors) and teachers, to equip the saints for the work of ministry, for building up the body of Christ." **Eph. 4:11-12**

These churches are not governed by a Senior Pastor, staff, and board of directors but by elders and deacons, father and mother figures, and regional or area leaders that are sometimes called "uncles." Individual churches are not a single organized gathering with a pastor, a building, and a set of unique or denominational rules and programs. Instead, they are more the organic and interwoven fellowship and community of

Christians in a City or Region – similar to what we see addressed in the New Testament letters to churches. For example, the Church in Ephesus, the Church in Corinth, the Church in Laodicea, etc. The church in each region is the sum of all members of interconnected house churches, cells, and interdependent church gatherings.

Connectedness happens through their belonging to Christ and to each other. The church is centered around their earthly home: the common region or city. Unity is practically expressed in house churches and cell groups that are linked together, as well as large celebrations wherever possible, or at least regional leadership meetings in areas where the church is being watched or persecuted. For example, a comparatively small church planting network in one area in China, would count 400,000 attendees. The larger networks number in the several millions. The 10 largest regional (not national) church planting networks in China, Vietnam or North-India would completely change the list of the largest megachurches. Now that's exciting!

So far, we've considered form based on size and structure. In the next chapter we'll look at other considerations.

Reflections

What's your preference? Think about the size church where you are most comfortable.

_____

_____

Now consider and ask God, does that feeling of comfort come from your own preferences or is it because that's what you believe God has in mind for you with regard to using your gifts and calling to benefit His Church and expand His Kingdom?

_____

_____

What kind of leadership structure do you prefer?

_____

_____

What kind of leaders does God endorse and support according to scripture? See I Timothy 3 and Titus 1:5-9 for clues.

_____

_____

Are you that kind of person?

_____

_____

Chapter 16
Forms Are Flexible

W hile we were discussing the need for church reform a friend once remarked, *"Things always revert to form without pressure."* That's true in the natural world and in the church. I believe we're in one of those inflection points in history where Jesus is applying the pressure necessary to build His Church in such a way that the Church of Jesus Christ is without spot or wrinkle at His appearing, just as His Word predicts. Perhaps you too feel the pressure. While often uncomfortable and perhaps sometimes downright painful, the heat and pressure God is allowing, indeed that He is applying, will eventually produce a good result if we just hang in there long enough to see it.

For centuries, the forms of Church around the world have been varied and quite remarkable. From the early days of meetings in synagogues surrounded by the trappings of ancient Jewish tradition, to the houses, caves, and gatherings outside of towns due to persecution, to State endorsed and controlled churches, cathedrals, spires, and stadiums, the places of meeting, the seating, decorations, and ornaments have all served the Church of Jesus Christ in one way or another. The multitudes of prayers, praises, scriptures, and sermons lifted in over 7000 living and dead languages still ring in the ears of God and the hearts of people connecting them in holy communion. Not the same at all in our estimation, but still one in God's purpose.

Whether seated, standing, on our knees, or even on our faces before God, we worship Him in Spirit and in truth. Do we differ in many ways? Yes. Are we one in the sight of God? Yes.

Over the course of the Church in the world there have been splits, divisions, denominations. Even in the Eastern Orthodox Church that considers itself "pre-denominational" there are fifteen self-governing councils of churches and several more that are related. Many of these divisions have occurred due to differences in preference and beliefs regarding one church form or leader over another. Despite what you may have heard, joked about, or believed; church splits are not a God ordained church growth strategy. In one of His last recorded prayers Jesus beseeches His Father in **John 17:11**, *"And I am no longer in the world, but they are in the world, and I am coming to you. Holy Father, keep them in your name, which you have given me, that they may be one, even as we are one."*

Does that mean everyone in the Church is to be exactly the same? Same doctrinal understanding, same practices, same language, same social status, same ethnicity, same politics? The Word of God does not indicate that anywhere. Jesus was in human form as He prayed this prayer, yet He and the Faither and the Spirit were always one. When He prayed this prayer His disciples were already beginning to include Gentiles. His life, relationships, teachings, and practices varied from the life, relationships, teachings, and practices of the Pharisees, Sadducees, and the Sanhedrin. No longer would God's chosen saints be confined to Jerusalem or even Israel. The Church would become a worldwide movement. Could the forms of organization and practice of individual churches be different while maintaining the oneness that Jesus intended?

Let's look at the Church in Antioch as an example. **Acts 11:20-26**. *"But there were some of them, men of Cyprus and Cyrene, who on coming to*

Antioch spoke to the Hellenists also, preaching the Lord Jesus. And the hand of the Lord was with them, and a great number who believed turned to the Lord. The report of this came to the ears of the church in Jerusalem, and they sent Barnabas to Antioch. When he came and saw the grace of God, he was glad, and he exhorted them all to remain faithful to the Lord with steadfast purpose, for he was a good man, full of the Holy Spirit and of faith. And a great many people were added to the Lord. So Barnabas went to Tarsus to look for Saul, and when he had found him, he brought him to Antioch. For a whole year they met with the church and taught a great many people. And in Antioch the disciples were first called Christians."

The church was conceived in Jerusalem. God empowered them on the Day of Pentecost. From Jerusalem the Gospel spread rapidly, with churches springing up throughout Asia and the Roman Empire. That was a transformation of form.

With persecution in Jerusalem and the dispersion of the apostles and believers, the church in Antioch began to take on greater significance than the church in Jerusalem in terms of church growth, church practice, church government, Christian missions, and even matters of biblical theology, where issues like circumcision, the Law, and salvation were debated and settled. It was in Antioch, where large walls literally separated the city into Greek, Arab, African, Syrian, and Jewish quarters that God began to do an amazing thing. Jesus broke down these barriers as people were saved and came together to worship Him. They were literally called the first Christians. Jesus unites people together as one in His body.

In another important form shift, the role and status of women in both culture and the church changed significantly. Jesus accomplished this in more than one way. Some of it was already at work in the Gentile world due to Greek and Roman secular influence. But through His Church, Jesus elevated the status of women to a new level.

Jesus had women disciples from the beginning of His ministry. They were there when he traveled, preached, taught, and performed miracles. They were there when He was crucified. They were witnesses to His resurrection. They were in the Upper Room at Pentecost. Throughout history women have been instrumental in the witness, the testimony, and the work of the Church. Thru His life, death, and resurrection Jesus forever reset the status of women in the world back to God's original intent, establishing through the Church and in society the OT truth that women are not property; they are co-heirs of the grace of God and are to be treated with dignity and respect. Equals with men in the Kingdom of God and in the Church of Jesus Christ. Even a cursory reading of scripture provides evidence that the role of women in the early church of the New Testament was significant and substantial. To be true to the heart and testimony of Jesus, that's a truth with application to church form that is worth revisiting in the Bible again and again.

The face and form of the Church continues to change worldwide. Changing demographics and church forms will certainly have a significant impact on how we do church. According to the Pew Research Forum, in 1900 Europe and North America made up 82% of the world's Christian population. By 2005, Europe and North America only held 39% of global Christianity, with Africa, Asia, and Latin America making up 60%. By 2050 it is projected that 71% of the Christian population in the world will reside outside of the US, Canada, and Europe.

What does this mean to the Church in the Western world? For one thing, the demographic picture of America is changing. America has always been a diverse nation. The city where I live, Durham, NC is more diverse than much of America. Durham wasn't as upended by the civil war as many other southern cities. In fact, the last surrender of a major Confederate army in the American Civil War occurred in Durham. The history of Durham is the story of black, white, Jew, and more recently Latino, Asian, African, and others working and living alongside each other. Durham certainly has its problems, but Christians here recognize

God's hand in gathering people literally from every race, tribe, tongue, and nation to our city for His purposes.

In the 1970's a word from God reached the United States and eventually our city that issued from the largest megachurch in the world in South Korea. The message was of a large revival that would affect the United States and eventually many parts of the world. According to the word that was delivered by an ordinary believer in a cell group with no connection with our part of the world, this revival would begin in Durham, NC. The churches in our city are still waiting and praying to see if this is a true word from God because it hasn't happened yet. We do not know how this will turn out, but we certainly believe God can do it. Hope in God does not disappoint.

One good thing that has already occurred since that word was delivered is that many churches with different forms from several streams have come together for years to watch and pray. For more than two decades pastors from more than forty churches, representing different ethnicities, congregations, denominations, and generations meet weekly for prayer for our city. We have held city-wide prayer events that gather wonderfully diverse groups of believers. From my experience, travels, and discussions with pastors in other places it seems that is remarkable. Sometimes we overlook the present work of God while we are looking for something else that we hope or expect to happen at some point in the future.

What do we mean by "revival?" The Church has experienced many God-ordained occurrences of this type through its history beginning with Jesus. **Rom. 14:9 KJV**, *"For to this end Christ both died, and rose, and revived, that he might be Lord both of the dead and living."* Revival occurs when spiritually dead people come to new life in Jesus. I've had the privilege of both receiving salvation during such a time and being an active participant and minister as it occurs in other places.

Typically, when revival happens among people living in a certain city, region, or nation the dividing walls of race, culture, social status, generation, and denomination come crashing down. When that occurs, the forms of church that people have been comfortable with necessarily change as multitudes of newly saved people come alive in Christ and are adopted into His family, the Church. When large-scale revival hits, every church meeting and building that is available is not adequate to meet the need for the Church to gather. The form of our single day worship services as we presently know them will not be adequate or even desirable when God calls His people together.

It is the responsibility of the universal Church made up of individual churches to take these new believers in and make Jesus disciples. We should begin now to examine our forms with faith that God will continue to save others just as He saved us. We must be ready and able to labor and minister together with other brothers and sisters in Christ. How will we relate to Christians that are dedicated to a different form of Church than ourselves? How will they relate to us? Will we be able to surrender our preferences to Jesus and walk together in obedience to the Head of the Church?

As a pastor my constant prayer was, *"Oh God, make this church a church that looks like (our city) Durham."* What did I mean? I wanted Jesus to so gather our congregation that we would represent the population at large in every way including gender, age, ethnicity, tribe, language, and national citizenship. We want to be an expression of the Church that is prepared to deliver the Good News to the entire community. If the Church is going to be relevant to the communities where God has chosen to place us and to our world, we would be wise to seek God in preparation and be willing to change our forms as He directs.

Please hear my heart. I am not advocating social engineering for the sake of the Gospel. Some of that has happened in the name of God and it has been a disaster. Our best intentions may not be of God at all. We must have the mind and the heart of Jesus. Then everything else becomes a matter of obedience to His will. We must be open and willing to change the form of the church as God desires. To do anything less is sin.

When we honestly look at the state of the Church in the USA today (not just our own congregation, stream, or denomination) we are faced with a gloomy picture of the church in decline, with less people being born again with each generation. The Church at large in both our own country and around the world has widely lamented this fact and perhaps prayed that God would do something to change the situation. I personally know that Chinese "uncles" have been praying for God to bring persecution to the American church to cleanse and purify her for decades. Thanks, Chinese brothers!

We may not be praying and making that request, but many American Christians are certainly praying that God will do something to reverse the trend away from faith in Jesus. Here's the good news! He is already answering our prayers. It is happening.

To see it we have to look, not at what some define as "church growth" which is most often just moving sheep from one pen to another. The church in America actually is growing, at least in one key segment. Where is that? Primarily among immigrants and particularly among undocumented immigrants.

According to PEW Research of the approximately 11.1 million unauthorized immigrants living in the U.S. during the last survey conducted, an estimated 9.2 million (83%) are Christians, many from Latin America. If Jesus is indeed in control of His Church, it would be reasonable to wonder whether He is moving faithful brothers and sisters in Christ to the USA to face a legal immigration system that is difficult if not impossible to navigate? That doesn't even begin to address the enthusiastic evangelism of believers from other nations within and without their own communities that often leads to the making of even more disciples.

Perhaps this is the hope and the future of the church in the US and the Western world. What if many of the refugees from the Middle

East and North Africa that are currently in Europe turn to Jesus? How would that change the Church there? Western churches have not generally invested labor and resources to cultivate and harvest these fields of immigrants. Many arrive in America and Europe after being forced to flee from countries after wars, severe ethnic, tribal, and religious persecutions, and other dangers. As an example, Muslim immigrants fleeing war, famine, and physical danger often respond to genuine extensions of concern, kindness, assistance, and friendship from Christians.

I am concerned that much of the Western church is way behind the curve in terms in coming to grips with what God is doing. The rise of immigrants is already the future of our nation and the Western world in general. According to an old 2008 US Census Report, *"minorities, now roughly one-third of the population, are expected to become the majority in 2042. By 2050 the nation is projected to be 54% minority. By 2023 minorities will comprise more than half of all children."* New census data analysis provided by the Brookings Institute in 2020 concluded that the nation is diversifying even faster than predicted. That's significant to Christians and nonbelievers alike.

In terms of the message of this book, here's the most important news: the majority of these newcomers are either already Christian or may soon respond to the Good News once it is presented in a culturally appropriate manner. While internal and external surveys show the church in continual decline in America, they are only a snapshot of the situation as it exists now, or more likely as it existed some years ago. They are not an accurate indication of the future. The church is alive and well in America, just not among majority white and majority black churches where growth is stagnant. With the growth of immigrant Christians and new converts, the Church is poised to mount a major expansion of the Kingdom of God both in the West and around the world.

Why don't many Christians and churches see or acknowledge this trend? Rather, some fight against it. Could it be that God wants us to examine and perhaps change our forms to conform to what He is currently doing to bring people to saving faith and make disciples? It's not like that has never happened in the history of the Church.

We can see some indications of how the strain over changing form was played out in the US Episcopal Church's decision to ordain homosexual priests and bishops. I'll leave it to the reader to consider why the leadership of the Episcopal Church made the decision to change form and practice in this manner. Whatever the reasons, it sparked a strong response within the Worldwide Anglican Communion. For example, the African Episcopal Church took a more conservative view of the scriptures that caused a reckoning in the denomination. In worship style African churches tend to be livelier, more active in evangelism, more communal in shared ministry in the church and to their community, with strong discipleship programs that place obedience to Christ over the authority of an individual's personal choice. African Episcopals elevate the authority of the Scripture ascribed to Jesus over traditions, forms, and practices established by church hierarchy. For these reasons some American Episcopal churches realigned themselves with the African Episcopal Church. As a result, the form of their churches also changed.

As I write this the same dynamics are playing out in the United Methodist Church. That's my heritage and I'm watching and praying with great interest.

I have a friend that is pastor of a congregation belonging to the Nigerian church in America. Nigeria is a nation with a strong religious fault line that runs between the Muslim majority in the north and the Christian majority in the south. Adherents of both faiths often deal with religious tension and strife that can become quite extreme. This sharpening of faith and practice has refined the form of the Nigerian Church. Immigrants from Nigeria come to America with the unique form of their churches intact and the results are dramatic. Prior to the restrictions of COVID prohibiting large events the Nigerian Church in America held their annual convention, not at one of the larger congregation's facilities or in a hotel convention center, but in Madison Square Garden. It was standing room only and people were lined up outside watching on screens and worshiping in public, unable to gain entry.

When you attend a church that has its origins in Latin American you will experience fervent, communal prayer, exuberant worship, standing in silence and reverence when the Bible is read publicly, attention to intense spiritual regeneration and training, lively preaching, and teaching, with instruction and hands-on discipleship in Christian living for new believers. After the service you are likely to remain for some time enjoying a hearty meal and lots of love and fellowship around the table. The communal meal is considered a normal component of worship. We experienced the same thing in a church in Germany that was primarily populated with Italian and other immigrants where wine was provided to accompany the excellent cuisine. That tweaked our American church sensibilities.

Yet so far, the Church in America has primarily stayed within our own ethnic community boundaries. That's why we speak of white churches, black churches, Asian churches, Latino churches, and so on. Some of it has to do with the desire to worship in a common language in the comfort of shared culture, likes, dislikes, interests, and values. There's nothing inherently wrong with that unless preserving our human culture has become more important than the work of God. King Jesus has His own set of values for His Church. There's a culture of the Kingdom of God and it is wonderfully diverse, supportive, and creative. Every now and then we see breakthroughs where churches with different forms come together to commonly worship, pray, and work for the Gospel in a city or region. For those that can hang with it, the experience can be wonderful.

Sociologists tell us that there is a third culture emerging in America; the next generation of people from American and immigrant parents that, while honoring their cultural traditions and shaped by them, they are not bound by them. These third culture Christians see a much different future for the Church than the one their parents or grandparents have known. They see a Church that is unified out of necessity because they live in a broader American culture that is increasingly hostile to the Gospel. In the current generation of American-born Christians that grew up knowing only more traditional forms of church I can't help but wonder, will there be an openness to explore and perhaps join the third culture generation in seeking the Lord for His will?

My years in ministry with experiences in different nations, languages, and cultures leads me to believe there is a Kingdom culture emerging in the church today that is not just occurring in America. It is a global phenomenon that takes the only form that matters, the form of Jesus Christ.

The Bible informs us this time is coming, ready or not. Perhaps now is the time.

"Beloved, now we are children of God, and it has not appeared as yet what we will be. We know that when He appears, we will be like Him, because we will see Him just as He is."
I John 3:2

What will it take for believers everywhere to reach this destination foretold in Bible prophecy by the return of Jesus? Perhaps our current church forms contain spots and wrinkles that are currently being washed, scrubbed, and pressed out by God to produce a Church that is holy and blameless, ready to present to Christ in all her glory. If so we should not despise the work of God but rather embrace it.

In the next chapter we'll see where the Church is headed and how the story ends.

Reflections

Think of the form or forms of church you are familiar with. What are the strengths and weaknesses?

_____

_____

_____

_____

_____

How do your personal preferences for church align with God's Word and the prophecies of scripture?

_____

_____

_____

_____

How might you need to change to conform yourself to God's plan for the Church?

_____

_____

_____

_____

_____

Chapter 17

The Victorious Church

My early experience has forever influenced my thoughts about Jesus, God the Father, the Holy Spirit, and the Church. When you're caught up in a sovereign movement of God and nearly all your friends and social acquaintances come to Jesus in short order, it definitely has an impact on your life. It's not an experience that you just get over. Most of my friends have remained faithful to Jesus and served Him more or less faithfully for over fifty years. We still share a bond that is hard to explain to other people. My wife is constantly amazed at the relationships we have maintained over a sizeable distance all these years. I realize it isn't the normal experience. It's something that God did, and it has endured. One of the songs we regularly sang was, They Will Know We Are Christians by Our Love. The first line is, *"We are one in the Spirit, we are one in the Lord."* Turns out, that was true.

We were in love with Jesus because He loved us first. As a result, Jesus imparted His love for our brothers and sisters in Christ and for people that didn't yet know or understand the Good News that Jesus is Lord. When you love someone, other interests fade into the background. Dividing walls fall down. The church doesn't have an organizational or even a theological problem. The church has a love problem. Too many have fallen out of love with Jesus and with His people.

If you study spiritual awakening and revival movements in history, you'll soon learn that young people are almost always the first to be affected and catch the wave. As we get older, we seem to become more set in our ways and less inclined to notice and pay attention to the Spirit of God when He is at work in ways that we may not understand or appreciate. As an old acquaintance that was saved during the Welsh revival of 1904-1905 used to say, "Pity." Truly it is. When we become blind to the work of God by the Spirit to challenge and reform churches that have outlived the usefulness of their form, or that have abandoned the person of Jesus and obedience to the Holy scriptures to serve another philosophy or idol, God will not tolerate that. He will move as necessary to ensure salvation for all those that will call upon His Name.

In Revelation 2 Jesus speaks to seven churches. Some believe these letters represent the church throughout the Age of Man prior to the return of Jesus. The first one that he addresses is the church in Ephesus. Is that the early church? Perhaps. He commends them for their work, their endurance, and their persistence in rooting out evil and doctrinal error. Then He says this in **Rev. 2:4**, *"But I have this against you, that you have abandoned the love you had at first."*

Jesus then warns them that unless they repent of this and do the works that are once again the result of love for Jesus and love for others, He will *"remove your lampstand."* In other words, Jesus will remove this church as a holder of light, His light. When a church no longer exhibits the love of Jesus, God is not pleased, and He will bring it to an end.

Today there are many people that once called on the name of Jesus and made the commitment to faithfully follow and obey Him. In doing so some ran into a church culture that was not faithful to love Jesus and love people as He does. Fortunately, that's not the end of the story. **II Timothy 2:13**, *"if we are faithless, he remains faithful—for he cannot deny himself."*

If you're reading this because you have pain, disappointment, and grief in your soul from your church experience, Jesus has good news for you.

> *"A BATTERED REED HE WILL NOT BREAK OFF, AND A*
> *SMOLDERING WICK HE WILL NOT PUT OUT, UNTIL*
> *HE LEADS JUSTICE TO VICTORY."*
> **Matthew 12:20** *cf. Isaiah 42:3*

Fortunately, Jesus is the Head of the Church. **Ephesians 1:22-23** says of God the Father, *"And He put all things in subjection under His (Jesus') feet and gave Him as head over all things to the church, which is His body, the fullness of Him who fills all in all."*

What is the outcome when the church is the Church as Jesus intends? Jesus said that He will build His church and the gates of Hades will not prevail against it. The Church of Jesus Christ is by definition a victorious, overcoming spiritual body consisting of God's people. The Church is a witness and a visible testimony of the nature, the character, and the transformative, almighty power of Jesus Christ. What does the victorious Church look like?

As we've learned, we can't define the victorious Church based on the form it takes. There are many great and grand cathedrals all over Europe and Latin America that are dead and devoid of the Spirit. Drive around my hometown or any other in most of America and you'll likely see great and grand church buildings that are either empty, lifeless, and powerless, or that have been converted for other uses. No matter where you are you'll find a group of people that methodically gather and call themselves a church, yet they meet without the presence and the authority of Jesus Christ, and without the unction of the Holy Spirit, because there is no commitment to God's authority, no obedience to Jesus, to His Word, and to His love. Zombie churches.

How do we find a victorious, overcoming church as it exists today? Once again, our reference is the Bible. In this section we're going to look at a lot of Scripture. Through circumstances that I do not remember I came across an Asian church leaders' list of characteristics that describe the victorious church. While I cannot quote the source, I find it to be helpful. These characteristics are not listed in order of importance, and again, I'd be hard pressed to rank them. It appears the Bible gives them equal weight and value. A victorious church today is:

1. A church that experiences the power of the Holy Spirit daily – **John 6:63**, *"It is the Spirit who gives life; the flesh profits nothing; the words that I have spoken to you are spirit and are life."* This will happen corporately. People are saved, baptized, discipled, filled with the Spirit, the presence of God is evident. It must also happen individually. Our lives should be filled with supernatural encounters, experiences with God, divine direction, and the Spirit's guidance.

2. A church that experiences the true fellowship of the Body of Christ – **Acts 2:42-47**, *"And they devoted themselves to the apostles' teaching and the fellowship, to the breaking of bread and the prayers. And awe came upon every soul, and many wonders and signs were being done through the apostles. And all who believed were together and had all things in common. And they were selling their possessions and belongings and distributing the proceeds to all, as any had need. And day by day, attending the temple together and breaking bread in their homes, they received their food with glad and generous hearts, praising God and having favor with all the people. And the Lord added to their number day by day those who were being saved."* This should be the norm. We must not so easily explain away why this does not apply anymore. **I John 1:7**, *"but if we walk in the Light as He Himself is in the Light, we*

have fellowship with one another, and the blood of Jesus His Son cleanses us from all sin."

3. A church that knows the Bible and accurately and effectively practices and uses it – **Eph. 6:17** tells us that, *"the Word of God is the sword of the Spirit."* **II Tim. 3:12-17**, *"Indeed, all who desire to live godly in Christ Jesus will be persecuted. But evil men and impostors will proceed from bad to worse, deceiving and being deceived. You, however, continue in the things you have learned and become convinced of, knowing from whom you have learned them, and that from childhood you have known the sacred writings which are able to give you the wisdom that leads to salvation through faith which is in Christ Jesus. All Scripture is inspired by God and profitable for teaching, for reproof, for correction, for training in righteousness; so that the man (anthropos) of God may be adequate, equipped for every good work."* People in the church will be involved in scripture reading, study, memorization, and practical application.

4. A church that is serious about evangelism – **Matt. 28:19**, *"Go therefore and make disciples of all the nations…"* **Mark 16:15**, *"Go into all the world and preach the gospel to all creation."* **Romans 10:13-15**, *"for "WHOEVER WILL CALL ON THE NAME OF THE LORD WILL BE SAVED." How then will they call on Him in whom they have not believed? How will they believe in Him whom they have not heard? And how will they hear without a preacher? How will they preach unless they are sent? Just as it is written, "HOW BEAUTIFUL ARE THE FEET OF THOSE WHO BRING GOOD NEWS OF GOOD THINGS!"* Declaring the Good News will be both corporate and individual.

5. A church that is committed to serving the needs of society – **Matt. 25:35-40**, *"For I was hungry, and you gave Me something to eat; I was thirsty, and you gave Me something to drink; I was a stranger, and you invited Me in; naked, and you clothed Me; I was*

sick, and you visited Me; I was in prison, and you came to Me.'
Then the righteous will answer Him, 'Lord, when did we see You
hungry, and feed You, or thirsty, and give You something to drink?
And when did we see You a stranger, and invite You in, or naked,
and clothe You? When did we see You sick, or in prison, and come to
You? The King will answer and say to them, 'Truly I say to you, to
the extent that you did it to one of these brothers of Mine, even the
least of them, you did it to Me.'

This is the faithful Church throughout history. It is always the church of Jesus Christ that is here to demonstrate the love of God in practical ways, to lift people up and light the pathway to truth and salvation in both its temporal and eternal forms.

The forward to the book *How Christianity Changed The World*, by Alvin J. Schmidt notes,

> *"It is has become politically correct to fault Christianity*
> *for authoritarianism and repression, a faith that promoted*
> *fanaticism and religious warfare while impeding science and*
> *free inquiry...the author clearly concedes its shortcomings...*
> *yet the evidence demonstrates that ...no other religion,*
> *philosophy, teaching, nation, movement – whatever – has*
> *so changed the world for the better as Christianity has done."*

Think of what the church has accomplished by the enabling of Jesus Christ and the power of the Holy Spirit. Millions of people's lives have been transformed by Jesus resulting in the common good. From the Church the sanctity of human life is established, the elevation of sexual morality, women receiving personhood, freedom and dignity for all people, children treated with love and nurture, the development of the scientific method, organized medicine, health care, hospitals, orphanages, schools, colleges & universities, aid organizations (Red Cross, Salvation Army, even the United Way was founded in 1887 by Christian leaders), the modern work ethic, the concepts of economic freedom, of liberty and justice for all, the abolition of slavery, the advancement of art and architecture, music, and literature, and the ongoing struggle to eliminate poverty and deliver people from oppression. The result is that the freedoms, prosperity, and the divine providence that we in the West and particularly in the USA take for granted have all come through divine providence, and the hard work and painful struggle of the Church of Jesus Christ at work in the world.

Today we have the great opportunity and the great challenge to represent Jesus Christ to the world and continue the work of His church no matter the opposition from the enemies of God and mankind.

1. A church that knows the strengths and weaknesses of the opposition – Satan's external and internal tactics, and uses the spiritual weapons provided by God to overcome and defeat the Devil. **I Peter 5:8-9**, *"Be of sober spirit, be on the alert. Your adversary, the devil, prowls around like a roaring lion, seeking someone to devour. But resist him, firm in your faith, knowing that the same experiences of suffering are being accomplished by your brethren who are in the world.* **I John 3:8**, *"for the devil has sinned from the beginning. The Son of God appeared for this purpose, to destroy the works of the devil."* This is what Jesus calls us to do as His body. The church moves against the devil with discernment, obedience, and the delegated authority of God.

2. A church that is self-supporting and free from outside power and control. When church and state marry, the church has the wrong partner. It never produces good fruit. We've seen this in the various nations of Europe. We're currently seeing it with Russian Orthodox hierarchy and Vladimir Putin. We're also experienc-

ing our own version of Christian nationalism with the alliances of Trump and Evangelicals, progressive churches and the Democratic Party. **II Cor. 6:14**, *"Do not be bound together with unbelievers; for what partnership have righteousness and lawlessness, or what fellowship has light with darkness?"*

The same could be said of any kind of dependence on anyone or anything but Christ. Even things that look good or seem to solve important problems. Our church has operated a community Food Pantry for more than forty years. At one time we accepted Government subsidies and grants. It was fine for a while. Then there were conditions. We were told we can't pray or proselytize. We were required to collect demographic information and report it to government agencies. Those things conflict with God's commands and the primary functions of the Church. We opted out. The Church must be discerning and remain dependent on God and independent of earthly masters, corporately and individually. Our politics, our ethics, and our sociological views must always submit in obedience to Jesus and to His Word.

3. A church that is bold and ready to witness even in the face of persecution. Think of Peter and John before the High Council in **Acts 4:12-13; 18-20.** *"And there is salvation in no one else, for there is no other name under heaven given among men by which we must be saved. Now when they saw the boldness of Peter and John, and perceived that they were uneducated, common men, they were astonished. And they recognized that they had been with Jesus....So they called them and charged them not to speak or teach at all in the name of Jesus. But Peter and John answered them, "Whether it is right in the sight of God to listen to you rather than to God, you must judge, for we cannot but speak of what we have seen and heard."*

Right now, this is the normal life of people of the Church in countries that are hostile to Jesus. I've been privileged to know some of them, to hear their stories, to worship with them, to see their wounds, and be challenged by them to likewise be bold in my own witness. It's uncomfortable and it is humbling, but it is also necessary. Will you and your church be ready when your turn arrives? Do you have a personal example in a friend or mentor that will encourage you? Does your church have anyone like that?

4. A church that is committed to shared responsibility – **Rev. 5:8-10**, *"When He had taken the book, the four living creatures and the twenty-four elders fell down before the Lamb, each one holding a harp and golden bowls full of incense, which are the prayers of the saints. And they sang a new song, saying, "Worthy are You to take the book and to break its seals; for You were slain, and purchased for God with Your blood men (Gr. Anthropos-men and women) from every tribe and tongue and people and nation. You have made them to be a kingdom and priests to our God; and they will reign upon the earth. "*

The Church has been provided structure in the Bible. God gives apostles, prophets, evangelists, pastors and teachers, elders, and deacons. There is order and there is delegated authority. But please read, observe, and seek application carefully, considering the whole counsel of God. The Lord never intended to create a clergy/layman class struggle, or to excuse "regular believers" from responsibility in the church. Men did that. The Bible says all believers are ministers of reconciliation and priests unto God. **Gen. 1:26**, *Then God said, "Let us make man in our image, after our likeness. And let them have dominion over the fish of the sea and over the birds of the heavens and over the livestock and over all the earth and over every creeping thing that creeps on the earth."* We all share that responsibility. **Eph. 5:17**

& 21, *"Therefore do not be foolish, but understand what the will of the Lord is...submitting to one another out of reverence for Christ."* We must use the delegated authority of God well, in the way that He intends.

5. A church that is a praying church – **Col. 4:2**, *"Devote yourselves to prayer, keeping alert in it with an attitude of thanksgiving."* The ESV translation renders the beginning of this verse, continue steadfastly; The Message – Pray diligently. **I Thess 5:17**, *"Pray without ceasing."* The NIV reads, pray continually. **I Tim. 2:1-2**, *"First of all, then, I urge that entreaties and prayers, petitions and thanksgivings, be made on behalf of all men, for kings and all who are in authority, so that we may lead a tranquil and quiet life in all godliness and dignity."*

A Pastor from Vietnam testifies that before he was imprisoned for Jesus he worked with prayer in the background. Sometimes he was too busy to pray. In prison he discovered the importance of prayer. He describes prayer now like a pilot using a checklist before he takes off. The first item on our checklist should always be prayer. If we skip it or minimize it the whole mission is in jeopardy.

In summary, **Romans 12:21** instructs us, *"Do not be overcome by evil but overcome evil with good."* This is what the victorious Church looks like in the world now. Better yet, there is an even more glorious kingdom coming. In the next chapter we'll examine the Ultimate Victory of the Church with the return of Jesus Christ. For now, please read and meditate on this passage before moving on.

Everyone who believes that Jesus is the Christ has been born of God, and everyone who loves the Father loves whoever has been born of him. By this we know that we love the children of God, when we love God and obey his commandments. For this is the love of God, that we keep his commandments. And his commandments are not burdensome. For everyone who has been born of God overcomes the world. And this is the victory that has overcome the world—our faith.

I John 5:1-4 ESV

Reflections

Does Acts 2:42-47 describe normal Christian life in a faithful Christian church today?

_____

_____

_____

_____

Why or why not?

_____

_____

_____

_____

Would you like to be part of a church that fits this description?

_____

_____

_____

_____

Why or why not?

_____

_____

_____

_____

Chapter 18
The Seventh Function

This book began as a sermon series. In chapter 10 I outlined six functions of the Church. I remarked that perhaps we'd discover a seventh and reach a perfect number. Numbers in Biblical times were often symbolic of a deeper meaning. The number seven is especially prominent in Scripture, appearing over 700 times. From the seven days of Creation to the many "sevens" in Revelation, the number seven connotes such concepts as completion and perfection, exoneration and healing, the fulfillment of promises and oaths.

I'm not a big Bible numerology guy, but the idea intrigued me. Earlier I asked if you could determine a seventh function? I asked the same during my sermon series. Mrs. Erna Bell Gordon (Ernie to her friends), our former pastor's widow, came to me before we reached the end and proposed a seventh function of the church. She's a wise woman of God and I've learned to listen to her. I want to introduce her proposed seventh function to you in this chapter. She concluded that one of the Church's primary purposes is:

7. To wait and watch for the visible and bodily return of the Lord Jesus to establish His rule and His eternal reign over all of Creation.

Seems obvious now, doesn't it? Thank you, Ernie. The Apostle Paul writes of this important Church function in **I Corinthians 15:50-58**. *"Now I say this, brethren, that flesh and blood cannot inherit the kingdom of God; nor does the perishable inherit the imperishable. Behold, I tell you a mystery; we will not all sleep, but we will all be changed, in a moment, in the twinkling of an eye, at the last trumpet; for the trumpet will sound, and the dead will be raised imperishable, and we will be changed. For this perishable must put on the imperishable, and this mortal must put on immortality. But when this perishable will have put on the imperishable, and this mortal will have put on immortality, then will come about the saying that is written, "DEATH IS SWALLOWED UP in victory. O DEATH, WHERE IS YOUR VICTORY? O DEATH, WHERE IS YOUR STING?" The sting of death is sin, and the power of sin is the law; but thanks be to God, who gives us the victory through our Lord Jesus Christ. Therefore, my beloved brethren, be steadfast, immovable, always abounding in the work of the Lord, knowing that your toil is not in vain in the Lord."*

This is what we work for, what we live for, what we watch and wait for. The Church of Jesus Christ is by definition the victorious, overcoming, worldwide gathering of God's people; the witness and the visible testimony to the nature, the character, and the power of Jesus Christ to transform lives and to overcome and ultimately destroy all the works of the evil one to the glory of God the Father. The Church of Jesus Christ on earth is the temporal, physical evidence that the Kingdom of God is real, and it exists among us right now.

Jesus said in **Matt. 11:12** (NIV) *"From the days of John the Baptist until now, the kingdom of heaven has been forcefully advancing, and forceful men lay hold of it."* According to scripture this waiting and watching for Jesus' appearing is not a passive endeavor. It is an active function of His Church from the time He ascended into Heaven until His visible return. **Titus 2:11-13**, *"For the grace of God has appeared, bringing salvation for all people, training us to renounce ungodliness and worldly* *passions, and to live self-controlled, upright, and godly lives in the present age, waiting for our blessed hope, the appearing of the glory of our great God and Savior Jesus Christ."*

The church today is certainly waiting on something; a salvation that has yet to appear. To many people on the outside, it looks like we're not particularly happy about it. You might wonder if the church has an inferiority complex? What do I mean by that?

Christians are often defensive and defeatist in our attitude when we feel challenged by anyone that questions our faith or treats us as if we are irrelevant, incompetent, or worse, a hindrance to the advancement of a modern and free-thinking society. Here's a hard question. Could there be some truth in that assessment?

Christians can sometimes individually and corporately be self-pitying and exhibit a great deal of self-loathing. If I had a nickel for every complaint I've heard from Christians about what the church is not, or what is wrong with the church, or why they don't attend church anymore, I'd be a very wealthy man. Some Christians lament the waning of power and influence that the church once possessed. Others wonder if we ever really had any, or even if we should. We treat the church, the gathered people of God, as if we are defective, as if we should be ashamed of our identification by default, guilty of some deep hidden and shared insecurity or collective sin. But that's not what God says in His Word. These are lies the devil sows that we have believed. How do I know that? The truth is written in God's Word. The scriptures state:

- That your sins are forgiven.
- That you are the righteousness of Christ.
- That where the Spirit of the Lord is, there is liberty.
- That there is now no condemnation in Christ Jesus.
- That God has not given you a spirit of fear, but of power and love and a sound mind.

- That He who is in you is greater than he who is in the world.
- That Jesus has become for us wisdom from God.
- That God will meet all your needs according to His riches in glory.
- That we can do all things through Christ who strengthens us.
- That God always leads us in triumph in Christ.
- That in all things we are more than conquerors through Him who loved us.

Read that list again, slowly this time. In **I Cor. 2:9** it is written, *"No eye has seen, no ear has heard, no mind has conceived what God has prepared for those who love him."*

That's true right now, here on earth. What do you think heaven is going to be like? We need to wake up from our apathy and discouragement. We need to shake off the blinders and the lies that we have accepted from false sources and have faith in God. Faith in Jesus and His Return is not stupid. Faith is not without reason. Faith is not the crutch of the mentally or socially deficient. Faith is the substance of things hoped for, the evidence of things not seen. Faith is real and it is tangible. In the Church, we can see it and experience it.

Jesus came once and completely upset the world. He lived a perfect life. He performed miracles. He showed us the Father. He is the Way we must follow, the Truth we must believe and proclaim, the Life we must experience and pursue for His glory. He died on a cross. He rose again on the third day. He ascended into Heaven. He promised He would return. Now 2000+ years later the Church He established and continues to build is without a doubt the most powerful force for the demonstration of God's goodwill on the planet.

Jesus has more disciples alive and testifying to His Lordship on the earth today than in all previous world history combined. Do you secretly think His Word is not good? Do you question whether He is coming back? Do you think His church is not triumphant? Do you think he will not have us ready to reign with Him for all eternity? If you believe any of these things, I recommend you prayerfully revisit the Bible and ask the Lord to reveal and confirm His truth to you. Ask Him to consume all the lies you may have believed and burn His truth into your mind, your heart, your soul, and your spirit. The time until His Return is short. This is important for you, for your brothers and sisters in Christ, and for the multitudes of people in the world today that are in desperate need of the real Savior. Too many people remain trapped in terrible circumstances, built on man-made philosophies, demonic ideologies, and false religions that hold them captive and threaten to pull them into Hell with the Devil and his minions. People need to know Jesus and His salvation.

"For 'everyone who calls on the name of the Lord will be saved.'
How then will they call on him in whom they have not believed?
And how are they to believe in him of whom they have never
heard? And how are they to hear without someone preaching? And
how are they to preach unless they are sent? As it is written, "How
beautiful are the feet of those who preach the good news!"
Rom. 10:13-15

I have spent decades praying for and working with brothers and sisters in some of the most difficult places on earth to be a Christian. In one of those countries the situation is so bad that they have ceased praying the way that we do. Here's a different church culture to consider. These brothers and sisters no longer pray primarily for their basic needs. They no longer pray first for their family and friends. They no longer pray just for a government and a leader that will no longer persecute them so harshly. They no longer even pray for their own health or even their own lives. What are they praying for?

When they are able to meet and in their private prayers, they pray first and most fervently that Jesus will return immediately. Every time they can gather, which is not often and never safe, this is the focus of their prayers. They pray this individually and they pray this corporately without ceasing. They have asked us in the Western church to pray with them. Will you join them in that prayer to support our persecuted brothers and sisters?

We too in the West are waiting, although perhaps not with the same sense of urgency. As we wait, we're charged to take back what the enemy stole from humankind in the garden. In **Isaiah 64:1** the prophet cried out, *"Oh, that You would rend the heavens! That You would come down! That the mountains might shake at Your presence."* God heard and answered that prayer. He did come down. Jesus came to earth and announced that people everywhere should repent because the Kingdom of Heaven is at hand. When He was crucified, the sky became dark and the mountains trembled as a witness. These things were written down and passed along to us by faithful witnesses in the Word of God. We can be certain that God's Kingdom is here even now. He is with His Church.

After the resurrection Jesus told His disciples that they would be His witnesses to the end of the age and the end of the earth. Then in Acts **1:11** He ascended into heaven and the angel announced, *"This Jesus, who was taken up from you into heaven, will come in the same way."*

I Thess. 4:16-17 says, *"For the Lord Himself will descend from heaven with a shout, with the voice of the archangel and with the trumpet of God, and the dead in Christ will rise first. Then we who are alive and remain will be caught up together with them in the clouds to meet the Lord in the air, and so we shall always be with the Lord."* These words, the true prophecy of scripture, are still speaking to His Church today – the victorious Church.

We must sometimes force ourselves to face certain truths and remember that we don't live in a never-ending age of darkness and evil. This is one of those seasons. Prior to Jesus' day the Jewish apocalyptic writings pointed to an age to come where the entire world would be completely under the control of evil. After several hundred years of prophetic silence and a lack of divine intervention they believed that had happened. It seemed that God had completely withdrawn from the affairs of the world, that salvation belonged only to a distant and unforeseeable future when God's Kingdom would come in power. They believed that in the present world they would only witness and experience sorrow and suffering. Today, many believers and many churches act like we believe that's true as well. That we're just here to suffer, waiting to see if Jesus returns.

In my own childhood Arkansas vernacular; that's hogwash. Feel free to Google it.

In reality, we live in an age of God's grace and mercy precisely because Jesus came just as was prophesied in the Old Testament. While He was with people on earth, He established His Church and proclaimed to His disciples that the gates of Hades would never prevail over it. If we believe that is true Christians don't have the right to be a pessimistic people. Yes, the Bible tells us that darkness and evil will intensify as we approach the end of the age. But the Bible is also clear that as the darkness increases, so will the light of Christ in the witness and testimony of His saints, His Church. We are not alone. We have not been abandoned to the power of the Evil One. Satan has already been defeated at the cross and through His resurrection. We win!

We end this chapter with our focus again on the Seventh Function – that we are to actively wait for the visible and bodily return of the Lord Jesus Christ. How do we do this? We stand together in the Church, forever changed by the radical, amazing, transforming power of the love of Jesus Christ that makes us different than we were before. Holy, anointed, set apart for God. We humbly bow to His authority over our lives. We submit ourselves in obedience to His plan, His purposes, His will. We commit ourselves not only to the Lord, but to each other – as fellow heirs of the Kingdom of God and the promise of His return to lead us forward in victory. We rejoice in our salvation. We give ourselves wholeheartedly to fulfill all seven functions of the church:

1. Evangelize
2. Make disciples
3. Minister
4. Fellowship
5. Worship
6. Demonstrate the wisdom & the authority of God
7. Wait and watch for the visible and bodily return of the Lord Jesus to establish His rule and His eternal reign over all of Creation.

As we wait for His return, we are reminded of God's challenge in **II Peter 3:11-12**, *"what sort of people ought you to be in holy conduct and godliness, looking for and hastening the coming of the day of God."*

You may say, "OK, but what am I supposed to do with that? What does that mean to me? What is my place, my purpose, my destiny? What am I here for?"

As we read in Hebrews 11 commonly called "The Faith Chapter" of the Bible, we could tell a thousand stories of what most people would call ordinary Christians that have done remarkable things for Jesus. In truth, there is no such thing as an ordinary Christian. As born-again believers, filled with the Holy Spirit of God, destined to live and reign with Jesus forever, we are all quite extraordinary.

I know a man from an unremarkable family. He had a normal childhood in middle America. His grades in school were unremarkable. He was not someone that stood out from the crowd in any way. When he was a teen, his life was transformed by the power of God, and he gave himself to Jesus Christ. At age 18 he moved to the Middle East and has never looked back with regret. He speaks, reads, and writes in several different languages. He has preached the Gospel in many different nations, to many different peoples and people groups, in some of the harshest place for Christians. He makes disciples. He plants churches. He has translated the Bible into another language and oversees the distribution of thousands of copies electronically and in hard copy. He has seen violent persecutors become followers of Jesus. He has also suffered dearly for his faith and the sake of the Gospel. He has now lived more than half his life in the Middle East. His work and dedication to reaching people for Jesus spans the entire region.

He once was ordinary. No one took notice or expected much from him. No one but Jesus. Jesus called him out. Jesus made him extraordinary. That's the Way of Jesus.

What is your purpose, your gift, your calling from God? That's a big question and one that is often hard to answer. Here's one way you can determine what God has in mind for your destiny. When you think of the various evils that actively stalk people, that prey on the weak, the helpless, the poor, the innocent, what moves you intellectually or emotionally? What stirs your soul? What horrifies you? What injustice angers you? What wrong do you feel the need to correct? What problem that violates the nature and character of God do you feel that someone needs to address and perhaps resolve? Where does the love of God call you to invest and engage?

The only truly effective way to address these sins, these evils, these plagues on humanity, is for people to be saved from them. Like all people even the worst person needs to be transformed by the grace, the mercy, the love, and the power of Jesus Christ. Jesus can do that, just like me and yourself and the many brothers and sisters in Christ.

What are you and your church doing to fulfill the functions of the Church? Have you submitted to Jesus? Are you filling your place in His Body? I referred to our church's Food Pantry. The volunteers that have staffed it have worked day in and day out seven days a week to meet the need for food for thousands upon thousands of people in our community for over forty years. Lest you think we must have a lot of people in our congregation, the church is made up of less than 200 people. These Jesus followers not only meet our guests' physical needs, they pray for anyone that wants prayer, and they give of themselves in many other practical ways to help those who come seeking assistance to find, not just the fulfillment of their need, but to find Jesus and His great love.

Lest you think I am bragging let me be quick to tell you this. Our church is not an outlier. How many churches put on Vacation Bible Schools, operate nurseries, schools, children's ministries, perform humanitarian and evangelism outreaches? Thousands in our nation. Millions around the world. How can you serve the Lord in these and other ways to fulfill the functions of the Church? On more than one occasion I have been with volunteers crying at our Food Pantry because of the great need of someone they just met. That's not all just human emotion. It has to do with the heart of God and His great love for people.

Have you ever wondered what your calling is? Do you love God and love people in the way He commands? When you see people that are in danger or in need, does it move you to want to do something? Perhaps that's your ministry. This is where the Church is necessary. You may feel like God wants His Church to do big things. He does. However, we can't do everything alone and we're not intended to. Jesus' disciples spent time together with Him. Jesus is building His Church in such a way for you to have people that are loving, caring, mature, and secure in their faith, possessing godly wisdom to confirm your calling and encouraging you to pursue it. When you see people the way that Jesus sees them and it stirs you to want to act, maybe that's your part in the great plan of redemption. You are called to be God's ambassador to that person, to those people, and to act as His agent. You're Christ's ambassador because you know that without your intervention more people will suffer, more people will die, and more people will go to Hell without knowing the great love of God.

Yes, we are the victorious church when we hold fast to our faith together and follow the commands of scripture. You have at least the spark of the light of Christ. Together with other faithful believers you can shine the light of Christ into dark areas where you might otherwise not go. It is our responsibility to shine that light, the light of the Gospel of Jesus Christ, into every dark corner of the world as God sends us. As you wait for His return, I urge you to answer His call to go into all the world, preaching the Good News to everyone, making disciples of all the nations, overcoming evil with good.

Together we are the victorious Church. And together we say, Amen, Maranatha, which means, Come Lord Jesus!

Reflections

Ask God to help you be conscious and aware of the people and the conditions that stir your heart.

_____

_____

_____

_____

_____

Ask Him to help you see where your place is in His Church.

_____

_____

_____

_____

Ask Jesus to help you be active and purposeful as you wait for His return.

_____

_____

_____

_____

_____

Chapter 19
The Engaged Church

A young man that I mentored came to me lamenting his struggle to effectively lead a small group. I asked him what he thought the problem was. He replied, *"People know when they're not going anywhere."* I told him I thought that was wisdom and encouraged him to pray and seek guidance from God for the purpose of the group.

How can you put the things you have learned during your time reading this book into practice? How can anyone who follows Jesus Christ live effectively as a faithful member of His Church in today's world and in the future? How can a church, the gathering of God's people make a difference in the lives of people as we experience the culture of the Kingdom of God here on earth? The answer is, the same way that the Church has always done it, by being committed to being the living witness of Jesus Christ in the world today. It's who we are rather than what we do.

Remember the story about the men from the Coptic Church in Egypt that were executed on a beach in Libya by ISIS? They each had a small cross tattooed on their right wrist. It is the visible identification for Coptic Christians. It also serves a very practical purpose. In Egypt churches must be careful about who they allowed to enter. There are guards at the doors to identify believers from terrorists. The cross is their mark of faith. They've learned the wisdom of this tradition the hard way from massacres inside churches.

When I was in Iraq, I was honored to meet with believers from the Assyrian community. Their language is Aramaic, the common language of Jesus and his friends. Their churches date back thousands of years to the time shortly after Jesus' resurrection. Assyrian Christians and other ethnicities in Iraq also have guards for their gatherings and require some form of proof of commitment to Christ for entry. One of the girls that assists with Bible production and distribution gave me a small, simple cross on a tiny chain as a gift for my wife. It is lovely in appearance, but it became precious when I learned the reason it is so small and simple. The cross is easily hidden under clothing and may be produced for entry to the church. No sworn enemy of Jesus and His family would ever wear the cross, even for the purpose of tricking and destroying infidels.

If we are living faithfully as disciples, as His Church, we should expect to experience increasing resistance and conflict from the devil and the world forces of darkness. It should not be surprising, and it really isn't all that spooky. It is just the reality we find in the Bible. The good news is that it is often during unjust conflict and oppression that we begin to see the Church as Jesus sees it, as it really is rather than as just another religious entity. After all, the Church is the representation of the supernatural Kingdom of God here on earth. As such, there are going to be some unusual experiences that we just can't explain.

And oh yes. There will also be suffering.

Romans 8:16-18, *"The Spirit himself bears witness with our spirit that we are children of God, and if children, then heirs—heirs of God and fellow heirs with Christ, provided we suffer with him in order that we may also be glorified with him. For I consider that the sufferings of this present time are not worth comparing with the glory that is to be revealed to us."*

Suffering. It is not the essence of the Church. It is not a function of the Church. It is not a form of Church. However, like the cross it is one of the common marks of the Church.

I Peter 4:12-13, *"Beloved, do not be surprised at the fiery trial when it comes upon you to test you, as though something strange were happening to you. But rejoice insofar as you share Christ's sufferings, that you may also rejoice and be glad when his glory is revealed."*

We probably all know stories of missionaries suffering for Jesus. We all know stories of churches and believers in other places suffering for Jesus. In the West we never expect it will happen to us. That's an unrealistic expectation. God did not promise we would never suffer. If anything, the Bible says just the opposite. It's one of those things we put out of our mind until we're forced to think about it. That's understandable. No one in their right mind wants to suffer. However, as it is one of the common marks of the Church universal and as the Bible has so much to say about it, perhaps we need to at least consider and accept the premise that even when we suffer for righteousness, Jesus is with us. He suffered unjustly in our place. He knows what it is like. He promises He will go through it with us when it happens. This all sounds very cozy and spiritual in the abstract. However, when it happens to you it gets real very quickly.

In writing this section I had to think about what suffering for Jesus means to me. I'll be honest, I wouldn't do well with torture. I like to think I have a high tolerance to pain until I get a hangnail or pull a nose hair. If I was tortured for information, I'm pretty sure I would sing like a bird unless Jesus supernaturally shut my mouth and took away my ability to speak or gesture. Well, that's not a comforting thought.

As I've traveled for the work of the Gospel I have been in a few tight spots. I've been threatened and chased by a guy with a machete. I've been threatened with a car bomb. I've been chased by guys with guns. I've been investigated, under surveillance, and interrogated by authorities. Once I was pretty sure I was going to jail. I've had curses pronounced on me by witches. I've been very sick in places with little medical care. I've been in other dangerous and difficult situations. Have I ever really suffered for the Gospel? No. I don't think so. Nothing like some of my dear friends. But one day it may happen. I pray if or when it does, I may be bold in Jesus and not fail in my faith and my witness. However, in real life that works better in our minds than it does in practice.

One of the organizations I work with recently held an international video conference and the theme was persecution. Participants shared story after story of serious, often violent persecution. One of our key verses was **II Tim. 3:12** which plainly states, *"Indeed, all who desire to live a godly life in Christ Jesus will be persecuted."* Everyone in that conference had likely read and heard that verse hundreds of times. Story after story reinforced the truth of it.

Then one of the speakers put it this way. He said, "unless your church is experiencing persecution you must wonder if it is a faithful church." Full stop. Read that again. Make of it what you will but coming from someone that has lived it and suffered much for the Gospel his understanding and experience of the truth of II Tim. 3:12 is not easy to dismiss.

The Apostle Paul traveled as a missionary and founded many of the early churches. He also spent a lot of time in peril and in jail. As an example, consider one account of Paul and his young companion Silas. The story begins after they traveled through present day Turkey, Macedonia, and then arrived in Greece. In a place named Philippi they are accused before magistrates of disturbing the city with their presentation and demonstrations of the Gospel of Jesus Christ. The story is found in **Acts 16:22-34.**

"The crowd joined in attacking them, and the magistrates tore the garments off them and gave orders to beat them with rods. And when they had inflicted many blows upon them, they threw them into prison, ordering the jailer to keep them safely. Having received this order, he put them into the inner prison and fastened their feet in the stocks. About midnight Paul and

Silas were praying and singing hymns to God, and the prisoners were listening to them, and suddenly there was a great earthquake, so that the foundations of the prison were shaken. And immediately all the doors were opened, and everyone's bonds were unfastened. When the jailer woke and saw that the prison doors were open, he drew his sword and was about to kill himself, supposing that the prisoners had escaped. But Paul cried with a loud voice, "Do not harm yourself, for we are all here." And the jailer called for lights and rushed in and trembling with fear he fell down before Paul and Silas. Then he brought them out and said, "Sirs, what must I do to be saved?" And they said, "Believe in the Lord Jesus, and you will be saved, you and your household." And they spoke the word of the Lord to him and to all who were in his house. And he took them the same hour of the night and washed their wounds; and he was baptized at once, he and all his family. Then he brought them up into his house and set food before them. And he rejoiced along with his entire household that he had believed in God."

That was then and this is now, right? Would it surprise you if I told you that I've heard similar testimonies from people in churches around the world that are happening right now? I have personal friends that have led their greatest enemies and worst persecutors to faith in Jesus after God demonstrated His Truth in a supernatural way.

In the church that I attend now and once pastored one sister was miraculously, surgically freed from Stage Four cancer much to the surprise of the Director of Surgical Oncology and avowed skeptic. I say it was miraculous because the surgeon told her husband and me the cancer just peeled away like cellophane once they opened her up. Astonished, the surgical team realized they got it all. He was left totally bumfuzzled with no logical explanation. We told him it was God and he admitted he couldn't argue with us.

More recently a man associated with our church was in the hospital in critical condition suffering from massive organ failure with little hope of recovery. The hospital urgently called and summoned his family on

Sunday morning because he wasn't expected to survive any longer. While they were still on their way to the hospital, he was pronounced clinically dead. But that wasn't the end. God brought him back to life as his family and the church prayed together at the same time. God literally raised this man from the dead.

My own father was saved when Jesus appeared to him and spoke to him about his need to repent of his sins and surrender his life to the Lord. My dad was not a mystical guy, but he swore this actually happened. I know many people in various churches and in many nations that have experienced personal encounters with Jesus either in dreams or visions that led to their salvation.

I have dear friends engaged in the work of the Gospel in difficult nations that have been threatened, imprisoned, tortured, poisoned, left for dead, and suffered great losses. Yet they carry on the work of God; brothers and sisters in Christ surrounding them in prayer and encouragement both in person and from afar. I've witnessed the love of God transform peoples' lives in remarkable ways, setting them free from all sorts of bondage to sin and death. Haven't you? If not, how are you willing to change to be part of that?

From the beginning the Church has been upsetting the forces of darkness and a world system of evil. As the time grows near for the return of Jesus the Bible promises that the Church, God's family, will face increasing opposition. However, it is just as certain that we will also experience the incredible, supernatural blessing of God, the joy of the Lord, and the grace of God to not only endure these present difficulties, but to overcome them.

What does that mean practically? How should any church proceed and act? What form should the church take? As we've discussed, the form depends on many factors such as location, social climate, culture, tradition, and most of all the determination of the Creator God who knows so much more than we do about His will, His plan, and His purposes. However, there are some things that each faithful expression of His Church will have in common other than suffering.

- The church must be unshakeable in its commitment to our Head, Jesus Christ.
- The church must be unshakeable in its commitment to His Word, the Bible, to be obedient to His clearly revealed will, and our commitment to hold each other together to that standard.
- The church must understand and be committed to maintaining the essentials of the faith.
- The church must understand and practice all the functions of the Church according to scripture.
- The church must hold our forms lightly. We must be flexible and willing to change in strategy and practice so that whatever the enemy fashions to stop or hinder the progress of the Church in preaching the Gospel to all Creation, it will be impossible for him to prevail.

For the church to remain unstoppable and overcoming, every part of the Body of Christ, each individual member, must be flexible and responsive to the movement and the guidance of the Holy Spirit. We must be humble and submitted to one another. We must not operate in the flesh, our own mind, will, emotions, or understanding. The enemy should not be able to anticipate our moves. We must always pray and seek God's will together, take our orders from Jesus, stand together firm in the faith, and obey Jesus at all costs.

The following set of biblical instructions from the book of Ephesians should be helpful to you regarding the culture and practices of any faithful church.

Ephesians 5:10-21, *"Try to discern what is pleasing to the Lord. Take no part in the unfruitful works of darkness, but instead expose them. For it is* *shameful even to speak of the things that they do in secret. But when anything is exposed by the light, it becomes visible, for anything that becomes visible is light. Therefore it says, "Awake, O sleeper, and arise from the dead, and Christ will shine on you." Look carefully then how you walk, not as unwise but as wise, making the best use of the time, because the days are evil. Therefore, do not be foolish but understand what the will of the Lord is. And do not get drunk with wine, for that is debauchery, but be filled with the Spirit, addressing one another in psalms and hymns and spiritual songs, singing and making melody to the Lord with your heart, giving thanks always and for everything to God the Father in the name of our Lord Jesus Christ, submitting to one another out of reverence for Christ."*

Reflections

How will you put what we have just reviewed into practice in your own life?

_____

_____

_____

_____

_____

_____

_____

_____

What responsibility, if any, do you have to help a church, or a group of churches live according to the instructions of the Bible?

_____

_____

_____

_____

_____

_____

_____

Chapter 20
Conclusion

A s I wrote in the beginning, I love the Church. Recently Pam and I attended the funeral of a dear woman who was part of our church for several years. As a young woman when she married, she and her husband attended the First Presbyterian Church. They raised their children there and it was the only church they knew until they were adults and out on their own. This lady was very well known in the community for her kindness and generosity, and First Presbyterian was the obvious place to hold her memorial service.

During the well-attended service both my wife and I kept feeling a sense of awe. The grand, traditional edifice with its stone and wood, stained glass, pews, and massive pipe organ made for a lovely setting. We sang well-worn hymns of our childhood with gusto, renewed understanding, and fervor. We easily repeated from memory the liturgical touchstones of our youth in the assembled congregation. It brought lumps to our throats and tears to our eyes. But this was not sadness for our departed friend. We knew where she was and that she was ecstatic to be with Jesus. This was something else.

In the modern church in America, we stress the relationship that we have with God through His Son Jesus Christ. Rightly so. We would

171

never be able to approach God otherwise. However, in our familiarity we sometimes forget that He is more than just a close friend that cares for us and listens with patience to our problems and complaints.

God is our Creator, the Creator of the Universe. He conceived and fashioned everything that exists. He is the unchallenged Ruler of all. Because of Him we live, and move, and have our being. God is majestic and awesome and completely unlike us. He deserves and commands our respect and our reverence. God was present in that sanctuary just as He promised because two or more were gathered in His name. Our souls responded with reverence and awe and an overflow of emotion as we considered the goodness, the greatness, and the love of God for our dear sister, and for all the saints now passed on into His presence for all eternity. It was a holy moment.

There is continuity in the Church among all the saints of God. In the Church we experience the fellowship of the "great cloud of witnesses" described in scripture that have preceded us into His eternal presence. In the Church there is the now and the not yet of the Kingdom, the knowing of Jesus intimately, and the promise that we are part of His family. In the Church we experience the communion of the saints, the forgiveness of sins, the resurrection of the body, and life everlasting. In the Church we stand with millions of others in our witness throughout the ages before a world that desperately needs to hear and know about the sacrifice, the love, the power, and the salvation we have come to know in Jesus Christ.

Do we need the Church? Oh yes. In the New Testament the Apostle Paul, the most effective church planter, overseer, and inspired author of scripture in the Bible, writes about the Church in his letters. He provides these instructions in **I Cor. 3:10-15**.

"According to the grace of God given to me, like a skilled master builder I laid a foundation, and someone else is building upon it. Let each one take care how he builds upon it. For no one can lay a foundation other than that

which is laid, which is Jesus Christ. Now if anyone builds on the founda-
tion with gold, silver, precious stones, wood, hay, straw—each one's work will
become manifest, for the Day will disclose it, because it will be revealed by
fire, and the fire will test what sort of work each one has done. If the work
that anyone has built on the foundation survives, he will receive a reward.
If anyone's work is burned up, he will suffer loss, though he himself will be
saved, but only as through fire."

There is no other foundation for the Christian Church other than
Jesus Christ. No matter how dynamic or charismatic the speaker, if
he or she is not constantly pointing people to Jesus, the Bible clearly
indicates that person is not operating by God's Spirit and they are not
God's anointed. When Paul writes of building on the foundation of Jesus
Christ, he is not just talking about what someone with a title or a pulpit
does. We may read this passage and think it applies to someone else;
the apostle, prophet, evangelist, pastor, preacher, teacher, elder, deacon,
Sunday School worker, VBS teacher, Bible scholar, or small group leader.
That is not indicated here or anywhere else in scripture. This instruction
is laid out in **verse 10**, *"Let each one take care how he builds on it."*

Each one? What does that mean? That's every believer. God wants
us to understand that by our thoughts, attitudes, and actions we are
either building up or tearing down the Church, the house of God with
His family.

So, do this – read the above passage from I Corinthians again and
put your name in these verses every time you see "someone else," "each
one" or "anyone." Really, do it now. It's important.

Now do you understand what this means for you? How serious God
is about this? Please remember, divisions in the Church are a direct result
of spiritual immaturity. It's time for the Church, each one of us, to grow
up into the fulness of Christ.

Next, to better understand what our individual participation means
to the Church at large, read **I Cor. 3:16-17**, the verses that directly follow

this passage. Every time you see "you" it is plural. As we say in the American South, "you" means "y'all" in this context.

> *"Do you not know that you are God's temple and that God's Spirit dwells in you? If anyone destroys God's temple, God will destroy him. For God's temple is holy, and you are that temple."*

Although this has individual relevance, it is not instruction for individuals. As you can see, this instruction is given to all believers, meeting, living, and working together as the family of God. Disciples of Jesus bear a serious and weighty responsibility to one another and to the universal Church. This is holy to the Lord. We are holy to the Lord. Anyone or any group that tears down and divides the Church, the Bride of Christ, may expect a swift response with serious consequences from God. The language God uses is not merely symbolic or hyperbole.

I knew a man that was in and out of a church on two separate occasions over the course of several years. On the surface he was a nice guy that seemed to love the Lord. He was well-versed in the scriptures and was an engaging speaker. Whenever he spoke to the congregation, he made it a point to speak well of the elders and pastor. Both times he started a Bible study in his home. Both times he gathered a dozen or more people to him. Then he subtly undermined the pastor and elders as men that were not as spiritual as he was. He led his little flock to believe that the church leadership was not listening to God or following His will. Then when he had gathered sufficient numbers and some financial support, he told everyone in the congregation he was leaving to start his own church and invited anyone that wanted to come and join him. Those close to him followed as did a few others who were swayed by his appeal.

Both times these startup churches crashed and burned. Both times the people that left with him not only lost their faith in him, but they also lost their faith in the Church, and eventually their faith in Jesus. To my knowledge none of them returned to any community of faith. They were like wounded, lost sheep wandering here and there in search of food and shelter, afraid even to accept help and comfort when offered.

The first time this happened the pastor allowed him to return to the original church. Seeing his giftedness and believing the best of him and his meager apology, the pastor extended grace and mercy, hoping for his redemption. The second time he attempted a return the elders talked the pastor out of taking him back again. Still, he had supporters outside the church and sympathizers within, people that saw him as a good Christian man, perhaps someone even called to pastor and teach, even if his leadership character was flawed. From my perspective it was heartbreaking trying to follow up on people that were left broken, hurt, and disappointed by these experiences. They wanted nothing to do with any church or with God anymore.

The original church pastor was a dear man with a great big heart. He loved God and he loved people, even those that did him wrong and sought to harm him. So, when this man was diagnosed with the sudden onset of a life-threatening disease the pastor of the church asked me to go with him to the hospital. I went obediently if not enthusiastically. People had gathered to pray for this man and provide emotional and spiritual support for his wife and family. When I saw him lying in the bed, I knew he was near death. The only recourse otherwise was a miracle. The room was full of people and the nurse told everyone the family could stay but the rest of us needed to go to the waiting room.

We gathered there and people began to pray for a miracle. The hyper faith, "name it and claim it" movement was in favor at the time. Someone proposed that we hold hands and claim his healing by faith. Immediately a feeling of resistance filled me. I was never a hyper faith guy and this seemed particularly wrong, as if we were uniting to command God to do the will of the group. I asked God what He would have me do.

People hear God's voice in many ways. Mostly the Lord speaks to me either by bringing scripture to my mind or speaking to me in a still, small voice I hear in my inner being. However, this time the Lord spoke forcefully in a way that I could not miss. In fact, when I heard His commanding voice in my head, I looked around the room to see if anyone else heard it. I quickly recognized it wasn't audible, but it certainly seemed that way. God said very clearly to me,

> *"Do not pray that prayer. He did violence to My Bride and I will not tolerate that from anyone."*

This agrees with **I Cor. 3:17**, *"If anyone destroys God's temple, God will destroy him. For God's temple is holy, and you are that temple."*

It scared me so badly that I literally began shaking. I experienced the truth of the verse, *"The fear of the Lord is the beginning of wisdom,"* with new meaning. I got out of my chair and left the room as fast as physically possible. I walked with purpose down the hall, took the elevator to the lobby, and walked out the front door before I even paused to think about what to do next. One thing I know from this experience; Jesus is serious about His Bride, the Church. Maybe this is what is meant in **Deut. 4:24**, *"For the Lord your God is a consuming fire, a jealous God."* He will not long allow control of His Church to be usurped by another. The Church belongs to Jesus. He is in love with His Bride, with us. This is not to be taken lightly.

All true Christians have the same God, the same Lord Jesus, the same Holy Spirit, the same Bible. As God's family we have been given the greatest gift of all; forgiveness of our sins and salvation in Jesus Christ. The Holy Spirit distributes a multitude of spiritual gifts for the building up for the Body of Christ. But like two toddlers in a room with one toy (an example my pastor used often with great effect) in our mere humanity sometimes we refuse to grow up, and we fight over the prize of Christ's Church. Sometimes we even split it apart. That's not OK with God.

Let me just say in plain terms what God is saying through Paul in First Corinthians. Pride in divisions and denominations is not God's will. Those walls need to come down. Separating the Church by class, race, and ethnicity is evil. Those walls need to come down. Exalting one Christian leader over another and pledging allegiance to them to the exclusion of others is idolatry. Men abusing, controlling, and manipulating the lives and well-being of people in the church as if they are God is wicked. It all needs to end.

Paul pleads with the Corinthian Church and with His Church today in **I Cor. 1:10**, *"I appeal to you, brothers and sisters, by the name of our Lord Jesus Christ, that all of you agree, and that there be no divisions among you, but that you be united in the same mind and the same judgment."*

Still, this appeal often falls on deaf ears for those that are not ready to hear it. We're so used to the worldly system of division, strife, and power that it bleeds over into the church. We no longer even see strife and division in the church for what it really is: wicked, sinful, evil, dishonoring to Jesus, very serious to God. Division in the Church bears the imprint of Satan's work, and it must cease before Jesus returns. What is our responsibility in the work that Jesus is doing in building His Church?

Jesus said in **Matt. 18:6**, *"but whoever causes one of these little ones who believe in me to sin, it would be better for him to have a great millstone fastened around his neck and to be drowned in the depth of the sea."*

What are we teaching our children by our words and our actions? What will they make of our willing indifference to Church? Or worse, our resistance to the Church that Jesus is building? What message are we sending to our brothers and sisters in Christ that are different from us? What does the world see when they look at the church as an example of what Jesus is really like? Is Christ divided? Do we follow different leaders? Do we hop from one spiritual tribe to another hoping to have some insatiable need met? Do we selfishly and willfully refuse to grow in love, wisdom, revelation, knowledge, and understanding that might just change our preferences and traditions? Or worse, do we hold what we count as the wisdom and superiority of our own culture, race, ethnicity, gender, generation, political party, denomination, or tribe over the wisdom of God?

As Ephesians 4 indicates it is time to put these childish things aside and follow Jesus Christ, the Living Word. It is time to come together, to invest our lives with brothers and sisters in Christ, to grow in faith, to go where He leads us, to feed ourselves and others with Good News, demonstrating the life of Christ so that they too can be saved and grow with us into the fullness of Jesus. **I Cor. 3:21-22** tells us, *"So let no one boast in men. For all things are yours, whether Paul or Apollos or Cephas or the world or life or death or the present or the future—all are yours, and you are Christ's, and Christ is God's."*

Let's call these attitudes about Church and the resulting divisions what they are – sin. Let's lay down our pride, our divisions, our prejudices, our preferences, and put them on the altar of sacrifice to the Lord Jesus Christ. His Church is one holy temple, the dwelling place of God in the Spirit, with no place for division, bitterness, jealousy, or strife.

To do this together we must be willing to open ourselves up with faith and trust in God. We must be willing to open our hearts, our homes, and our congregations to those who have been grievously wounded by misguided churches and church leaders. We must offer the grace, love, mercy, forgiveness, and healing of Jesus to all who are struggling and even to our enemies. We must be willing to trust God and work with Jesus as He builds churches where all may truly come.

What is Church? There are many more things I could say and write but it is time to sum this up.

Church is the Love of God Expressed in Community

So simple yet seemingly so difficult to accomplish. And indeed, it is impossible were it not for Jesus and the power of His resurrection.

By the end of the New Testament the Church that Jesus established through the Apostles had already become multiethnic, multiracial, multinational, multicultural, and multigenerational. I'm reminded again of the lyrics of the song we sang passionately and earnestly when I was first saved. *"We are one in the Spirit, We are one in the Lord."*

One day the following prophecy regarding the Church will be fulfilled. **Rev. 7:9-10**, *"After this I looked, and behold, a great multitude that no one could number, from every nation, from all tribes and peoples and languages, standing before the throne and before the Lamb, clothed in white robes, with palm branches in their hands, and crying out with a loud voice, "Salvation belongs to our God who sits on the throne, and to the Lamb!"*

The Church was and is the living witness that the Kingdom of God exists now, here on earth. The Church of scripture is made up of Jew, Gentile, Roman, Greek, Asian, African, and Arab. It consisted of people from every known nation and tribe. The Church crosses all socio-economic barriers – male and female, elders and children, married and single, wealthy and privileged, middle class, poor, beggars, slaves, free, criminals, jailers. The people that make up the Church in the Bible come from a variety of political parties, alliances, philosophies, and occupations. There are business owners, leaders, and workers, members of trade guilds, government, military, civil servants, civic leaders, religious rulers, reactionaries, revolutionaries, refugees, the marginalized, and the oppressed. Disciples of Jesus come from various religious backgrounds-Judaism, paganism, sorcery, mystery cults, Greek and Roman mythology, idol worship, nature worship, and emperor worship.

As we've noted, the role and status of women in both culture and the gathering of the people of God changed significantly after Jesus. Their testimonies and relationships advanced the mission and influenced others to follow. They helped fund his work. Women were there when He was crucified. They were the first witnesses to His resurrection. They were in the Upper Room at Pentecost. Women hosted churches in their homes and carried Holy Scripture between cities. Women are instrumental in the witness, the testimony, and work of the Church throughout the ages.

In the way He lived His life, the way He publicly and privately treated women with equal dignity and worth, the way He died as they watched and mourned, and the way He announced His resurrection Jesus forever reset the status of women in the world back to God's original design and intent. He reversed the curse of sin. We are made in His image, male and female. Through the Church the Lord is still demonstrating the eternal truth that women are not property or to be considered as less than. They are co-heirs of the grace and salvation of God and are to be treated with the dignity and respect that is due daughters of the Most Sovereign Lord.

You can read how all of this was lived out in the story of Acts, but this is not just ancient history. The early Church that Jesus established was merely setting the stage for the grand plan of God being accomplished in the world today. In the Church we witness the wonderful diversity of God gathering and uniting people created in His image. In the Church we are reconciled to God through His Son as one Body of Christ. The Holy Spirit empowers us corporately with differing gifts, abilities, talents, and callings to reach as many people as possible for Christ, to provide evidence of His Kingdom, and to prepare the world for His Second Coming.

The Church is above all God's divine plan. No human could have come up with the idea of Church. We can hardly describe it much less make it happen in such a way to cover the earth with God's glory. The Apostles are sometimes credited with its origin by Jesus' detractors. No doubt they were remarkable individuals that spent time with Him and were commissioned by Him. But they were not special visionary organizational geniuses that somehow managed to construct an idea that could fool the world for thousands of years, much less transform the lives of billions of people.

Though clearly not manmade, the church incorporates the love, grace, mercy, justice, power, and wisdom of God in a way that somehow involves the cooperation of people. Yes, Apostles and people of the early church in scripture but also everyone that has walked and is walking the same path of faith. Today, the Church consists of people like you and me, who out of gratitude for what Jesus has done for us still seek His heart, His will, His kingdom, and then live and act in obedience to His commands. The composition and working of the Church are supernatural in the truest sense. What an adventure awaits us!

I have written this in the hope of lifting your eyes beyond what you can see in the natural world, to what God is doing in the supernatural. For those that have never been part of the Church, maybe this is where you belong. It is certainly where Jesus would like for you to be. For those that are in the Church but wonder what it is all about, I hope this inspires you to press in and seek Jesus with all the saints. For those that have been mistreated, misjudged, wounded, shamed, and harmed by churches, leaders, and members that have failed the vision and purpose of Jesus, I pray this book restores hope and encourages you to try again. This time you may be more confident in your understanding, with eyes wide open. Please know that wherever you stand in your relationship with Jesus at this moment, He is always there with you and for you. His arms are ever opened to embrace and love you into His presence.

There is so much more that could be written but this is what I have for you. As I said in the beginning, I love the Church and I hope you have been inspired to do the same. It's what Jesus would want.

I'd like to end with the lyrics of a song the Church has sung since it was introduced in 1866. It was one of my favorites as a child. It still is. I hope it will become one of yours.

The Church's One Foundation

The church's one foundation
Is Jesus Christ her Lord;
She is his new creation
By water and the Word.

From heaven he came and sought her
To be his holy bride;
With his own blood he bought her,
And for her life he died.

Elect from every nation,
Yet one o'er all the earth;
Her charter of salvation,
One Lord, one faith, one birth;
One holy name she blesses,
Partakes one holy food,
And to one hope she presses,
With every grace endued.

Mid toil and tribulation,
And tumult of her war,
She waits the consummation
Of peace forevermore;
Till, with the vision glorious,
Her longing eyes are blest,
And the great church victorious
Shall be the church at rest.

Yet she on earth hath union
With God the Three in One,
And mystic sweet communion
With those whose rest is won.
O happy ones and holy!
Lord, give us grace that we
Like them, the meek and lowly,
On high may dwell with thee.

Words: Samuel John Stone, 1866.

Music: 'Aurelia' Samuel Sebastian Wesley, 1864.

Setting: "Order of worship for the Reformed Church in the United States", 1866.

Copyright: public domain.

Thank You

Thank you for reading my book and taking this journey with me. I hope and pray that you have found your answer to the question, What is Church? My ongoing prayer is that you'll find and join a church that faithfully follows Jesus, celebrates and worships Him in loving community, works with Jesus to both live and share the Good News as He builds His Church, and actively waits with hopeful anticipation for His Return.

I'd love to read your comments and walk this important journey of faith with you. You can continue to connect with me and send me messages via my website, dubkarriker.com and by reading my blog posts and commenting at dubsteps.net.

I am eternally grateful for your time and interest. May you be richly blessed you as continue your quest for truth and meaningful relationship with the living God and with the people you encounter along the way.

Until next time, your friend,
Dub

About the Author

Dub Karriker is a retired pastor, current board member and leader of church networks, international ministries, and nonprofits focused on sharing the Good News, teaching, mentoring, and training. Combining his love of God and the Church with a passion for people and business, Dub also has a distinguished career in business operations with regional, national, and international corporations.

Dub is actively involved in a weekly prayer gathering of ministers in Durham, NC. He serves as a mentor to pastors, churches, and young believers. Dub and his wife Pam travel extensively focused on teaching, training, encouraging, and supporting oppressed people and Christians in difficult parts of the world. Dub and Pam have been married for forty-four years. They were licensed foster parents and are still blessed to serve as spiritual parents and grandparents to many.

Dub speaks and teaches at churches, conferences, and seminars domestically and internationally. His works have been translated into several languages. Dub's social media presence includes Facebook, Twitter, Instagram, and his dubsteps.net blog. He'd love to hear from you.

A free ebook edition is available with the purchase of this book.

To claim your free ebook edition:

1. Visit MorganJamesBOGO.com
2. Sign your name CLEARLY in the space
3. Complete the form and submit a photo of the entire copyright page
4. You or your friend can download the ebook to your preferred device

Morgan James BOGO™

A **FREE** ebook edition is available for you or a friend with the purchase of this print book.

CLEARLY SIGN YOUR NAME ABOVE

Instructions to claim your free ebook edition:
1. Visit MorganJamesBOGO.com
2. Sign your name CLEARLY in the space above
3. Complete the form and submit a photo of this entire page
4. You or your friend can download the ebook to your preferred device

Print & Digital Together Forever.

Snap a photo

Free ebook

Read anywhere

Printed in the USA
CPSIA information can be obtained
at www.ICGtesting.com
JSHW020240151223
53835JS00002B/6

9 781636 982199